YOUR TIME

— WITH THE —

BATON

YOUR TIME
— WITH THE —
BATON

WINNING THE RELAY RACE
OF FAMILY WEALTH STEWARDSHIP

STEVE BRAVERMAN

Advantage | Books

Published by Advantage, Charleston, South Carolina.
Member of Advantage Media Group.

ADVANTAGE is a registered trademark, and the Advantage colophon is a trademark of Advantage Media Group, Inc.

Printed in the United States of America.

10 9 8 7 6 5 4 3 2 1

ISBN: 978-1-642254-13-6 (Hardcover)
ISBN: 978-1-642254-53-2 (eBook)

LCCN: 2022912943

Cover design by Matthew Morse.
Layout design by Amanda Haskin.

This publication is designed to provide accurate and authoritative information in regard to the subject matter covered. It is sold with the understanding that the publisher is not engaged in rendering legal, accounting, or other professional services. If legal advice or other expert assistance is required, the services of a competent professional person should be sought.

Advantage Media Group is a publisher of business, self-improvement, and professional development books and online learning. We help entrepreneurs, business leaders, and professionals share their stories, passion, and knowledge to help others learn and grow. Do you have a manuscript or book idea that you would like us to consider for publishing? Please visit **advantagefamily.com**.

CONTENTS

ACKNOWLEDGEMENTS

My own "relay race" has been full of coaches, teammates, and those who have cheered me on.

To my dad, who has empowered me and given me the space and opportunity to explore so many of life's opportunities, I thank you for the "concrete safety net" beneath me.

To my incredible wife, Veronica. Running this leg with you alongside me makes every day full of love, laughter, and joy.

To Heather and Julia. Seeing you as I come around the curve, feeling your encouragement and excitement for a life full of hope and promise, I celebrate you and all the wonderful things ahead.

To Matt and Allan. Together with you as the "gas, brake, and engine," I am beyond grateful for your partnership, and I could not be more proud of what we have helped build together at Pathstone.

I hope everyone who has the opportunity to read this book and consider their own leg of their race will find a way to define and celebrate their legacy, and that we can together enjoy a better world for us all.

CHAPTER 1

THE GREAT WEALTH TRANSFER AND YOU

During the next quarter century, the United States will experience the largest transfer of wealth in modern history. According to the financial consulting firm Cerulli Associates, over the next twenty-five years, forty-five million households will transfer an estimated $68.4 trillion to the next generation.[1] If your household, your family, is among those participating in that transfer, there are a lot of things you need to think about—because doing it well will affect the lives of the people in your family, their descendants, and the life of our society as a whole. This great wealth transfer can only be improved by intelligent dialogue and an objective perspective on how to make that transfer effectively. This book provides that perspective.

On top of the current great wealth transfer, we find ourselves in a dynamic world of entrepreneurship within the younger generations

---

1   "The Great Wealth Transfer," Cerulli Associates, November 29, 2018, https://info.cerulli.com/HNW-Transfer-of-Wealth-Cerulli.html.

that is rewarding some of them with significant wealth. New innovations, new businesses, new opportunities, and new fortunes are being created every day, and if you are one of the people enjoying that new wealth, you also need to begin thinking about how and to whom you will pass on your wealth. It takes real thought and consideration to make it work well. I have learned a great deal about the dynamics of wealth transfer from my personal experience as an inherited wealth recipient, as the manager of my family's wealth, and as the CEO of Pathstone, a wealth management company with approximately three hundred active wealth management clients.

An acquaintance of mine told a story about someone he knew who worked in the private wealth management department of a bank. He once had a family that was so contentious about the wealth being passed on to them that, after days of fruitless wrangling among them, he had to lock them in a room at the bank and tell them he wouldn't let them out until they settled their differences! Wealth transfer does not have to be—and should not be—like this. It can and should be a team effort, like a relay race (more on that later) that takes into account the needs, wants, skills, dreams, and passions of everyone involved.

A lot has been written about the nuts and bolts of wealth transfer, and rightfully so. If $68 trillion is going to be passed on, people need to know about the legal entities, the trust vehicles, the rules and regulations. They need to know about estate plans, trust documents, complex asset allocation, investment policies that drive multigenerational investment portfolios, stipulating access to funds, and more— the cold hard facts of managing and transferring wealth. But there is a growing body of work on the "soft" issues around this, too, because, as we joke in the wealth management industry, it's the soft issues that are the hardest to deal with! I guarantee you that the people in that locked bank room weren't arguing about the nuts and bolts but about those difficult soft issues, about what should be done—or should have been done—with the wealth.

Soft issues include questions such as these: What is the meaning of wealth in my family? What are the family values; what is its culture? What do I want to achieve with my wealth for the family and for society? Now that I've created the legal structures with which to transfer the wealth smoothly, how do I establish an environment in which I can communicate effectively to the next generation my values, my culture, my perspective? So, it's good that we have a growing body of work about imparting knowledge and values to the next generation.

But I think it's more complex than that. Imparting knowledge and values is a one-way street. Maybe the next generation's values are a little different from yours; maybe they want to do things with wealth that you've never considered or do more of something that was also important to you. This is why the team approach that I advocate in this book is more effective, why it makes the soft issues not as hard to deal with.

The world is changing faster than ever, which means that the younger generation may be going places and doing things—or want to go places and do things—that the older generation wouldn't have done, and sometimes can hardly conceive of. That younger generation today is spawning new industries, new perspectives, new appreciations, and new goals, and they are taking on new challenges. The beneficiaries of that $68 trillion aren't going to just be dealing with a financial inheritance, but with a world that is moving even faster than their parents' world moved.

There are also changing family dynamics and demographics. Children are staying at home longer or more often returning to live at home. The younger generation is changing jobs more frequently. They often live in households that are less conventional than the family construct of the past. More of them are focused on social responsibility, on the idea of having a positive impact on the world, on changing the world for the better. In addition, wealth is often viewed differently in today's society than it was even a generation or two ago. The vision of families of stature and influence, families to be admired, is not as prevalent now. Sometimes there is even a social stigma around wealth, because of the social disparity, the wealth gap, that exists in society.

What does this mean for family legacies, especially long-established family legacies?

It means that the environment we currently find ourselves in requires that family conversations about wealth management and transfer go well beyond the concepts of what the trust vehicle is, what the financial metrics are. How does today's wealthy family in its totality think about its influence on society, about its culture, its perspective, its reputation? How does it deal with the very real fears that some wealthy people feel about inheriting wealth?

A recent Campden Wealth Limited study found that 54 percent of people who will inherit a considerable amount of money worry that they are going to lose that money, and 44 percent of those people worry that if they don't lose the money, their children will.[2]

This theme occurs in many conversations I have about wealth management. One person who was working on this issue told me, "I've learned tools to handle my fear of failure." Another said, "I feel empowered to peek behind the curtain and be more honest with myself about what I don't know and what I'm avoiding. I'm still not sure I'm asking all the right questions yet, but I'm starting to see what those questions are that I should be asking to learn more and be more competent."

---

2   *The Next Generation of Global Enterprising Families: Shaping Tomorrow, Today, 2020,* Campden Wealth Limited, July 2020, https://www.memberlink.net/system/files/survey/The%20 Next%20Generation%20of%20Global%20Enterprising%20Families%202020%20 %28002%29.pdf.

The Emotional Aspects of Wealth Transfer

So, even if you think you've established a good multigenerational asset-allocation plan, or a good trust structure, or a good legal contract under which to steward the assets being transferred, you still need to deal with the emotional aspect of wealth management and transfer. And this book will help you see that process in a way that takes that important emotional aspect into consideration.

The emotional aspect of this process deals with questions such as these: What if at the end of the day there is less capital, but there's a more enriched society or more fulfilled individuals in the family? What is the true legacy I want to pass on with my wealth? Is that legacy measured in dollars and cents, or is the legacy measured in personal and/or societal impact? Is it about future generations having a certain quality of life that keeps them well occupied, healthy, and fulfilled?

Here are things people I've worked with on these issues have said:

"I've been inspired to make change in my family, not by trying to change others but by looking inward to make my own personal development."

"I've learned more about how to relate with family members, and it's helped create better relationships. I also better understand healthy relationship dynamics and how conflict should be handled."

"I've learned to embrace my parents and appreciate them for who they are, not who I want them to be."

These are people who are taking seriously the emotional, interpersonal aspect of wealth management and transfer.

From my personal and professional experience, I have learned that wealth should be defined by far more than just the numbers, and that there are many areas to consider in order to create a successful legacy. This book is necessary because that massive train of wealth transfer is bearing down on society and is not going to stop. And dealing with this tremendous change is about a lot more than dollars and cents. This book is my effort to move people beyond the basics of setting up a trust. It's good that the industry has moved into having wealthy people impart information to their heirs to teach them, but, as I've said, that approach is one directional. Everyone involved in a wealth transfer needs to think about what the wealth means, what the family values are, why they want to pass the money on, and what those who receive it want to do with it. We need an ongoing dialogue among all of these people. Ultimately, all of these people will function best as part of a team, working together, listening to each other, learning from each other, and thereby making their team more successful and the individuals on the team more fulfilled—and, one hopes, also contributing to society in creative and lasting ways.

Wealth should be defined by far more than just the numbers

And if they do function this way, if each person stewards their wealth effectively, the family wealth will increase with each generation. For example, I have a client who inherited wealth and started a private company. He sold his private company to a public company and has a good deal of stock in that public company. He decided he wanted to sell off his stock to create more liquid wealth that he can use creatively. But as quickly as we sell off portions of this public company stock for him, that company's stock price continues to increase in value. And so it feels like he's never actually reducing his financial position in that public company.

The client challenged me to come up with a way to describe what's happening there that ties into wealth management. And I said,

"Well, you could say that it's a nice problem to have." But he didn't like that sentiment, so he asked me to come up with something else. I thought about it and I came back to the next meeting with the word *regeneration*, the way an octopus would regenerate a tentacle if it loses one. And he said that was closer but wasn't quite there yet. Finally, I realized that the right word was *opportunity*, because his position with this stock was creating new wealth that presented greater opportunities for him to be creative with his money. The client found this interpretation satisfying.

Creating new opportunities is what this book is about. Do the people with this family wealth want to build a business empire? Create more equitable workplace environments? Establish a charitable foundation? Figure out how to lessen environmental impact? What I'm talking about is multigenerational impact. One of the big things that is going to come out of perpetuating this team approach, this approach that involves partnership and collaboration, is wealth that will be measured not only by the perpetuation of the financial assets but by the continuity of a legacy, by creating fulfilled, satisfied, responsible individuals who care about themselves, their families, and their society.

Philanthropy can be part of it, of course. If you're going to give a large amount of money to a hospital and they're going to fund a study to cure cancer, that's wonderful. But the larger idea is to create a culture of wealth within a family that perpetuates personal self-worth, personal responsibility, maturity—in whatever ways different family members want to express those qualities. If your kids, grandkids, great-grandkids, and lineal descendants all find themselves fulfilled in their life's work, whatever that is, then what better legacy could there be for a multigenerational family of wealth? It doesn't just mean that each family member has received $X millions of spendable wealth. It means that they found a way to use the family's support to perpetuate their personal success and fulfillment.

When I was building my own business, with the support of my family's wealth, my kids watched me get on airplanes every week, sometimes missing their sports or drama events or whatever kinds of events they were participating in. But they understood—because I told them this as soon as they were old enough to understand it—that it was all about running my leg of the relay race, all about honoring the legacy I'd inherited from my father by striving to be successful. And now that my children are grown up, it's about me conveying to them that "I trust you, I honor you, I celebrate and support whatever you want to do with the wealth I've shepherded for you. I'm ready to partner with you. I'm ready to hear you."

If every generation in a wealthy family addresses the next generation with that kind of affirmation and support, the family will have a legacy of success. And, to me, that is the ultimate expression of successful wealth transfer.

Running the Relay Race

The way I like to describe wealth management and transfer to my clients is that it's like running a relay race. For me—and for my clients, too—this metaphor captures the process and the spirit in which we need to take on that process.

The stadium where the race is held and the track on which it is run is the world, the environment in which a family lives and the course they've chosen to run. You can't do a whole lot about the state of the world as a whole, but you can decide how you're going to run on that track, what your goals are, and how you want to pursue them in order for your family to cross the finish line a winner. Looking at the relay race historically, the first runner is the one who initially created the family wealth. That may have happened some time ago in your family, or you may be that first runner. The baton represents the wealth itself. The other runners are the generations to whom that wealth will be passed.

If you've ever watched relay races, you know that passing the baton is often the trickiest part. Many of them get dropped, making it impossible for the team to win the race. But even if the passing of the baton is smooth, each runner must know how to make the most of their strengths, and be passionate about how to run the race, in order to advance the baton as successfully as possible. When you or anyone else in your family is running their leg of the wealth race—working with the wealth they've inherited—they need to know their strengths and be passionate about how they're using the opportunity that this wealth provides.

In order to run a successful race, the teammates must help and support one another. The veteran runners must share their knowledge and provide support for the rookies. The rookies must be allowed to figure out what kind of approach to running their leg of the race will motivate and excite them, will keep them going when the running gets difficult. And usually teams need a coach to help them make the most of their potential. It's the same way with managing and passing on wealth—the experienced money managers in the family, and the coach, must educate the inexperienced members of the family, and they must allow those "rookies" to figure out how they can best employ the wealth being passed on to them, not dictate to them how to do that.

So, that's the overall metaphor for wealth management and transfer that I use, and now we'll look at each aspect of the race more closely.

You are a steward of your family's wealth management race. When you're handed the baton to run your leg, you are given the opportunity to use, develop, and hopefully increase that wealth. Just like a runner needs coaching and training to deal with the challenges that come up during a relay race—weather conditions, the state of the track, the behavior of opponents—you will require support and guidance to succeed at handling your inherited wealth, either from experienced people from within your family or from professional money managers outside of it, or both.

But, at the end of the day, it's your responsibility—and your opportunity—to run that leg of the race in a way that's personally fulfilling for you. However, you should always keep in mind that the baton, your wealth, isn't just yours; you're part of a team—your family—and the baton will be passed on to others. So, make the most of your time with that baton! As one of the people I worked with put it, "I've learned that each generation has an opportunity to be transformative in their own way."

By inheriting wealth, you're given a lead in life, and you're also given the opportunity to extend that lead for the next generation. How do you measure that lead? Dollars and cents? Impact on society? Successful perpetuation of the family legacy? It's usually some of all of these things, but when you get to the end of running your leg of the race, you're meant to transition to helping those who come after you to run the next leg successfully, to optimize their performance, to help them think through and adjust to any adverse conditions they might encounter.

In the wealth management and transfer process, if someone drops the baton, gets nudged off the track, or gets tripped up, you can be there to support them—the way a veteran athlete helps a rookie—by saying things such as, "Look, you're not using the best technique" or "Hey, I can show you how you lost your lead there" or "There are ways to ensure you don't get nudged off track." You can talk to them and help them along. (This is something the wealth management "coach" can do, too.) Veterans of dealing with wealth can share what they've experienced with the next generation, provide perspective, help them develop their own plan, and monitor their progress. You can share both the responsibility and the success. Because, in the end, what you're all aiming for is to get the whole family to the top of the podium, shaking hands and celebrating their victory.

The dialogue about wealth management and transfer should focus on the idea that each person's owning of the legacy, their running of their particular leg of the race, has to be built on that individual's talent, opportunities, and passions. A relay team has different people running different legs of the race because individuals have different talents and skills and preferences, and an intelligent relay race game plan takes advantage of what each individual has to offer. Wealth management and transfer should be handled the same way. By giving each individual the freedom, support, and power to map their own success, all involved will succeed.

Everyone needs to care about the success of the team. Veterans need to find the right way to empower people new to the game. Everyone needs to celebrate teamwork, working together. Everyone needs to celebrate victories and accept defeats when they come along— we win together, we lose together, we get up and run again when we fall, we adjust to changing circumstances. We do it all together. Using this approach gets you past the selfish concept that "this is my wealth, and I'm going to consume it until it's gone."

And that's my key message—a message that I've seen make a lightbulb go on in my own kids' heads. They get it. They've seen me run with the baton and extend the family's lead. They've seen the way I was empowered by family wealth. They cheered me on along the way and made some of their own sacrifices to give me the time to do that. They accepted what I was doing. And that made it easier to carry the guilt about sometimes missing their parent-teacher conferences or musical performances or athletic competitions. And my father cheered me on, too. So, the runners behind me and ahead of me in the race have my best interests in mind, as I have theirs. And my kids will be ready to take the baton and run their own legs of the race with the same kind of passion and dedication that I was able to put into running mine.

Now, it's true that I could have chosen to stand there with the baton and not extend the lead my father gave me, to not participate in the race. Some people have said to me, "Hey, Steve, you could have easily not worked and just enjoyed your wealth." And I could have. Because of my father's entrepreneurial success and his generosity to me, my family and I would have lived a very financially secure life.

But I wanted to do what my father had done. I wanted to perpetuate his legacy of growing the family's wealth and passing it on to my children—and, I hope, them passing it on to their children, and so on. The math suggests that I could have done nothing to increase the family wealth, but that would have evaporated the family "lead" not only financially but also culturally. It would have killed the energy that made my father successful and fulfilled, and I would have had no energy, no drive, no purpose, to pass on to my own children. And I am proud of his legacy—and mine.

Certainly there were sacrifices along the way. When I was a preteen, I noticed that my father was the one who was working hard all the time, working late, traveling, and so on. And, yes, there were plenty of dinners where he wasn't home and events where he wasn't around. But I knew what he was doing. He wasn't out on the golf course or hanging out at a bar. He wasn't traveling the world just for the sake of doing it. He was taking advantage of opportunities and building success. I came to appreciate that and ultimately wanted to emulate him.

For me, it was unintentional, at first, but then quite intentional. As he had done, I wanted to demonstrate for my kids that hard work brings real results and comes with real responsibility. My kids experienced that in a way that has allowed them to root for me. I made it clear that when I was there for them, I was there for them—fully. And when I wasn't there, it wasn't because I didn't want to be, but because there were other demands on my life. And I tried to balance those two things. You need the commitment of your family, you need your family behind you, in order to succeed in a way that is fulfilling —just like you need your

> *You need the commitment of your family ... in order to succeed in a way that is fulfilling*

team behind you to win your leg of a relay race. And my kids will have me behind them, just like I had my father behind me.

You don't want to fail your teammates in a relay race, because at the end of the day, it's a team win or loss. If you were handed a financial lead, go extend that financial lead. You were given an opportunity to find your passion, so find it and make the most of it. I celebrate all kinds of successes with my kids. But they are also prepared, are in position, to perpetuate and extend the lead that we have as a family. Ultimately, the way they extend that lead may not be financially measurable, but it's absolutely going to be measured in terms of their self-satisfaction, their sense of self-worth, their contribution to society, their values—the most important family legacy.

Why I Can Help You Run Your Race

Because we're dealing with a subject that will impact your life significantly—your fortune, your family, your legacy—I think you ought to know why I'm highly qualified to coach you about wealth management and transfer. A coach is someone who has worked with lots of individuals and teams—and has usually run races himself—so he has developed a wealth of knowledge about the most effective ways to do it. I've learned about wealth management and transfer from both the personal and professional perspective—through my own life experience and through working with hundreds of clients over the years. My personal story is a demonstration of an effective way to handle wealth management and transfer within a family, so I want to share it with you.

I started out observing my father as he followed his business passion to personal satisfaction and financial success, and I absorbed his values—he was the veteran competitor who taught me how to run the race. He was a savvy entrepreneur who followed his nose from one success to another, from becoming the largest importer of women's wigs in the United States in the late sixties—manufacturing them in Korea, where he was one of the largest private employers in the country—to founding Safeskin, the first company to manufacture powder-free hypoallergenic plastic gloves. (If you see purple or lime-green gloves in a medical setting these days, it's his product.) And there were other ventures in between. He would go from a concept to winning a leading global market share, all due to his entrepreneurial spirit and his belief in his own capabilities. He chose to take risks, but always well-thought-out risks, and he always worked with energy and passion. Naturally, this had an impact on my sense of how to operate in the world.

Dad and his board took Safeskin public in 1993, and the stock performed incredibly well. Harvard Business School even did a study of the enterprise's success. We sold the business to Kimberly-Clark in an all-stock merger in 1998, and they continue to manufacture the gloves under their sub-brand Safeskin. Dad took Safeskin from a concept to a multi-billion-dollar public company, and he took pride in that. But he told me that he didn't measure success in terms of his own personal balance sheet but in terms of the impact that success had on his employees. He liked to tell the story about one of those employees coming up to him at a company conference, pulling a photo out of his wallet, and saying, "Neil, I want to show you a picture. This is my house; this is my family. This is what's been made possible because of this job, because of the opportunity you gave me with Safeskin." Dad took real pride in creating such a positive impact on somebody else's life, let alone his own family.

I certainly took this to heart in my own business life, and his attitude resonates throughout our family. An important part of our family legacy is that we always want people to feel that they are better off for having known us, for having been involved with a Braverman enterprise, whatever that may be. The baton my father passed on to us included that attitude along with the family fortune. And that attitude will have an impact on everyone we in the family interact with over the course of our life. I've really worked hard to embrace the attitude that I inherited from my dad and impart it to my own kids. I try to live it with my partners and fellow employees at Pathstone, because I've learned that success is not only about measuring the dollars and cents but about measuring one's impact on the world.

Another important thing my father taught me was to follow my passion, to make my own way in the world. When I was a freshman at the University of Pennsylvania, Safeskin was quickly becoming one of the most successful medical glove companies in the world. And many people assumed that I would graduate and go right into the "family business." But my father was quite straightforward about my situation. He said he was proud of me for getting into an Ivy League school and told me to take advantage of the opportunity that this presented. He also said that I shouldn't go through college thinking that I was going to go to work in the family business. He said it was his responsibility to Safeskin to hire and engage the most technically savvy people, which wouldn't necessarily be me. He said he wanted me to know that while he was rooting for me, the fact that I had the same last name as him was not going to get me on a guaranteed glide path into that particular business. He advised me to find my own passion, develop my talent, and find an opportunity to employ that talent and passion.

I knew Dad would support me and advise me, but he was telling me to make my life what I wanted it to be. It was never specifically said, but it was always strongly implied that I could afford to be a material risk taker and that I ought to use that opportunity to explore what I really wanted to do in and for the world. So, he was saying, "Go make the best of this, do it with your eyes wide open, do it knowing that there's no guarantees at the end of the line—but also do it knowing that I believe in you as your father and that the family has been fortunate enough to provide you with this opportunity. So, don't settle." I think that "don't settle" is an important lesson to learn in life. A legacy should enable people to follow their passions, contribute to society, find self-fulfillment, and live a value-driven life. Don't settle.

Dad made it clear to me where we both stood and where we were both going. And it gave me a safety net that would allow me to explore and experiment with what I wanted to do with my life. I knew I could just take the baton and stand there, but that wasn't what

I wanted. I knew that wasn't going to earn his respect, the respect of my family, the respect of the world—or, for that matter, the respect of myself. I didn't want to just live off a trust fund; I wanted to advance the family's achievements and increase its wealth, not just live off what my father had created. I knew I could survive comfortably without working, but I knew I wouldn't be fulfilled following that path.

So, in college I focused on financial engineering and capital markets, because I enjoyed the math and the problem-solving and the fact that every day in the financial world is different. I enjoyed that it was a way to take on a question and find an answer, which was fascinating to me then and still is today. I guess you'd say it's a passion.

My education and my passion served me well. In my early post-college years, I leveraged an introduction from my dad to get into the derivatives business. I had worked summers during college as a runner on the Chicago Board Options Exchange, running trade tickets from the phone clerk out to the trading pit. I was a delivery person, the lowest rung on the ladder, but it gave me entry to the industry. I then leveraged that point of contact into an unpaid internship on the floor of the Philadelphia Stock Exchange. I was going to the exchange three days a week and going to classes two days a week at U Penn to finish my degree. I was a full-time student, but I organized my calendar so that I could spend maximum time on the floor of the exchange through graduation.

After graduation, in 1986, I leveraged my connections through the Philadelphia Stock Exchange to become a partner in a trading firm in Chicago and moved there. I was extremely well positioned from a derivative arbitrage perspective during the 1987 crash. So, as a twenty-three-year-old, I was fortunate enough to pull down a six-figure bonus. Eventually, I became a senior partner at a larger trading firm. I left that firm in 1996 and moved to the East Coast to found a division for a larger trading firm based in New York.

Ultimately, I bought out that organization from my partners and in 2000 formed my own trading firm, backed by family capital. We became one of the largest trading firms on the exchanges, with more than a hundred employees. Finally, in 2004, I sold that firm to a major financial services company, and it was at that point that I began to focus exclusively on managing my own family's wealth. I had told my dad that we ought to leverage my capabilities as a financial engineer to do private wealth management for the family. And he agreed. So, I essentially established the Braverman family office, although we weren't using that term in those days.

At that point, the family still had a concentrated stock position with Safeskin. We were in the process of redistributing wealth across the capital markets. As we monetized our concentrated stock position, we were constructing the trust that was the ultimate beneficiary of that distributed wealth. So I became a student on behalf of my own and my family's interests, because I was helping in real time with the construction of the family's investment portfolio and estate plan. Running a family office for my own family, I had to think about trust structures, multigenerational asset allocation, the balance sheet, philanthropy—all the things that wealth management and transfer entails.

Two years later, in 2006, my family was solicited as a client for wealth management by myCFO, a multifamily office started by Jim Clark, founder of NetScape and WebMD, and some associates. Allan Zachariah led this effort for myCFO, and we became good friends. Allan and I realized that we had the same philosophy about helping families steward multigenerational wealth. Ultimately, in addition to taking on my family as a client, myCFO invited me to become their president! So, like the guy on the old Hair Club for Men ads, I was a client, and I was running the company.

In 2009, I helped negotiate our exit from myCFO, lifting out the wealth management part of the business, and in 2010 completed the transaction that enabled Allan and me to establish Pathstone. I had to sign personally for the financial obligation of buying out our practice from myCFO to found Pathstone. We orchestrated our exit in a way that enabled Pathstone to be a start-up with a running start, because we had the support of clients, employees, and myCFO's parent company, the Bank of Montreal. Today, our company has about $40 billion in assets, fifteen offices, and one hundred equity-owning partners, and we are approaching 250 employees.

With Pathstone, I have found it exciting to have more problems to solve, more people to engage with, to leverage what I know for hundreds of families. And then, of course, it has been exciting to succeed at this, at something I'm passionate about, to enjoy success beyond just the adulation of my father and the gratitude of my own family, important as those are to me. Others were recognizing that I had something to offer, something that was valuable to them. I stay in touch with the day-to-day needs of my family, because I know the ins and outs of the family's wealth better than anyone I could hand that off to. But, at the same time, it is exciting for me to be able to demonstrate to my father, my wife, and my kids that somebody beyond the family appreciates my talents. This is why using family wealth to empower each member of the family to demonstrate their particular talents is so effective.

I hope this establishes that I know a great deal about the nuts and bolts of financial management and the transfer of family wealth. But I've also learned a great deal about the emotional aspects of this process. I've not only been through it with three generations of my own family, but I've also helped hundreds of other families through this process. And the intention of this book is to help any family who wants to understand the best way to manage and transfer their wealth.

CHAPTER 2

WEALTH OPPORTUNITY VERSUS WEALTH CONSUMPTION

Inheriting a great deal of wealth—being handed the baton—is akin to winning the lottery. Now, no one's going to whine about the fact that they inherited great wealth, but in the moment people celebrate their good fortune, there is also some dread mixed in. They recognize the tremendous opportunity that the wealth represents, but they also recognize that figuring out what to do with it, how to spend it, and how to steward it for their descendants presents a tremendous challenge.

In the 1950s, there was a television show called *The Millionaire* (back when a million dollars represented a lot more wealth than it does now) about a rich man, John Beresford Tipton, who had his assistant, Michael Anthony, present million-dollar checks to randomly chosen people. Then, the show would follow what happened to the people who got the checks. And it was not all good! It caused more trouble than it was worth for a good number of the recipients. This can happen to lottery winners, too (though certainly not all of them); the winnings can bring as much trouble as benefit. The main point of this is that these people were not prepared for the impact of great wealth on their lives.

A surprising number of families are not prepared for wealth transfer. According to the Campden study cited in chapter 1, "Just 50 percent of North American family offices have a succession plan in place ... Just 49 percent of succession plans are written." The top reasons given for the failure to do succession planning, besides the next generation not yet being old enough to deal with it, are

> **Grantors of wealth need to ensure that those they are passing the wealth on to are prepared**

"Not having a next generation member/s qualified enough to take over ... The patriarch/matriarch is unwilling to relinquish control ... [and] Discomfort in discussing the sensitive subject matter."[3] I will address all of these issues in this book.

Grantors of wealth need to ensure that those they are passing the wealth on to are prepared—which requires engaging in a dialogue about it. This is where the concept of the relay race and passing the baton is quite useful. If the wealth being passed on is presented as an opportunity to advance a family's standing in the world, to follow a passion or do good (and sometimes the two will coincide), it loses some of the stigma of conspicuous consumption often associated with

---

3   *The Next Generation*, Campden Wealth Limited, July 2020.

great wealth, the idea that wealthy people just spend, spend, spend on personal indulgences and luxuries. If people develop the sense that they are curating the wealth for their family, using it creatively and wisely so that they can pass it on to the next generation, a sense of purpose enters in, alleviating a lot of the stress that receiving a great amount of money can cause.

And this can be accomplished only if grantors of wealth are willing to engage in a frank dialogue with their inheritors about what the wealth will be and how the inheritors want to use it in their life. Too many grantors feel that just preparing the documents for the passing on of the wealth, the baton, such as setting up a trust, is the end of the process—but it's really just the beginning, because their inheritors need to be prepared to deal with the wealth. Grantors need to share what they have learned about managing wealth. If they don't, it's like putting someone into a relay race with no coaching or training! They'll be paralyzed, or they'll stumble and fall, or they'll be pushed off the track. The central purpose of this book is to get people to have the conversation, to have a conversation with the family about who you are and what the wealth means to you, and what the inherited wealth will mean to the inheritors.

The Purpose of Lane Lines and Referees

Sometimes grantors try to shirk their responsibility to work with the next generation by "governing from the grave," meaning that they set up an often very restrictive trust that puts the onus on the trustee to monitor the behavior of inheritors and distribute the wealth according to the wishes of the grantor, not the real-life needs and wants of the inheritors. Grantors will put language in the trust documents that seeks to both inhibit bad behavior and reward good behavior—but only as the grantor defines "bad" and "good."

For example, the grantor might put in a provision that inheritors will only get assets from the trust if they pursue "gainful employment." But what is gainful employment? Is it running a casino or opening a business, instead of being a schoolteacher or a member of the clergy? If there has been no dialogue between the grantor and the inheritors about this, and if the language of the trust does not reflect that dialogue, the poor trustee is stuck with trying to interpret what it means and enforce its provisions. So, it's important for grantors and inheritors to have conversations on subjects such as this while the grantor is still alive and lucid. If they don't, it's going to create a tremendous amount of difficulty for the trustee, because the trustee is bound as a fiduciary to follow the words of the trust as it's written.

More conversation now is better. Having conversations about wealth as opportunity versus wealth as consumption will create better outcomes than trying to orchestrate people's lives via a trust document. This approach will be more fulfilling and rewarding for both the grantor and the inheritors. It will enable the grantor, who is running their leg of the race—one hopes, in a satisfying way—to pass the baton smoothly to the next generation, so they can run their leg of the race in a satisfying way, too, a way that benefits the whole family. This approach will enable inheritors to pursue their passions, because the opportunity is there for them, not just a set of rules and restrictions about how they must live their lives. The idea of wealth as opportunity gets away from governing from the grave, because the grantor and inheritors talk about the future together now.

In this scenario, the grantor is saying, "Let me help you, let me guide you, let's establish a plan," instead of just handing inheritors a bunch of money—the result of which I discussed previously. The grantor coaches the inheritors and gives them the benefit of their experience, instead of laying it all on the trustee—which, under the wrong set of circumstances, can make things go sideways. The trust and the trustee can only bump the runner back onto the track when they go out of bounds, but otherwise the runner is on their own with little guidance.

Which is not to say that a trust with a trustee isn't important. You still need the structure the trust provides, and you need a solid, independent trustee. The structured trust is like the lanes painted on a racetrack—they guide the runner. The trustee is like the referee of the race. If you've got a good coach and the runners are well trained, the referee doesn't even need to be heard from. But the referee has to be there to make sure the runners stay in their lanes, follow the rules, and don't interfere with one another. If the grantor has had the discussions with inheritors that ought to happen, the trust document will be an expression of mutually agreed-upon rules about how the inheritance should be maintained and distributed.

A good trust document should afford the grantor the opportunity to set enough rules that they feel comfortable with it—the way a referee is comfortable with the parameters of a race, believing that the rules will be adhered to. But neither the trust nor the trustee should try to take on the role of the bad referee by overgoverning and interfering with inheritors' lives—and this won't happen if the trust is established with input from the inheritors. Then your trust will be there to provide a good structure, like the painted lines that keep the runners on course.

The Emotional Aspect of Wealth Transfer

I've been in the room with a seventy-year-old man who was hearing for the very first time that he was a centimillionaire, after living a very frugal life. The emotions he displayed were shock and awe—no joy. Of course, he had just lost his mother, but in addition to his feelings about that, you could see the fear and pain that this knowledge was causing him: fear, because his world was going to change dramatically, and pain, because he had not been prepared for it. He actually said to me, "Why didn't they tell me? Why didn't they trust me with this information? Why am I only hearing about this now?"

Wealth that is a multigenerational family legacy should all be about care and nurture and support and love. And in that moment, for that man, there was only disappointment and pain, the sense that his family hadn't trusted him, hadn't cared enough about him or thought enough of him, to tell him about this during his lifetime. I've never forgotten that moment, and the memory of it has shaped my approach to wealth transfer. This is what has led me to encourage grantors to embrace the conversation with their inheritors and make it about the opportunity of wealth, not the consumption of wealth, to make the wealth-transfer process a cooperative family experience, instead of a dictation from the grave.

If wealth is imparted to people without a plan, without vision, without taking into account the inheritors' passions, it can just feel like a burden. And this can lead to the inheritors feeling pressure to spend but having little sense of what to spend it on. Without a family dialogue, without engagement, without an appreciation by inheritors of the legacy and values of the family, you end up with lottery winner's syndrome—the feeling that life has gotten out of control and makes no sense anymore. If there is no conversation around what the family stands for and what the plan should be and how the grantor can help the inheritors find personal value and fulfillment, inheritors are just going to feel like somebody's handed them a big lottery check, and they have no idea of what to do with it.

It is well documented that, for most big lottery winners, once the euphoria wears off, having a huge amount of money feels like a daily burden. That's because the wealth is delivered without preparation, without passion and vision, with no sense of purpose behind it. If wealth comes into someone's life that way, they just feel like they need to get it off their back. I know that some people are going to read this and say, "That's ridiculous," but actual experience says otherwise. After the initial euphoria, and after you've filled your life with things, the wealth becomes something that owns you. And this whole concept of the relay race, of passing the baton, is meant to help inheritors not feel like slaves to their wealth, to help them figure out how to use their wealth creatively to give purpose to the rest of their life—to move past the concept of wealth as just money and move into the realm of value, growth, and personal satisfaction.

Far too many grantors of wealth spend countless hours sitting with their estate attorneys drafting the wealth-transfer document, and when they sign that document, they see it as the end of the wealth-transfer process. But that really should be just the beginning of the process. Imagine a coach throwing runners into a race with no training, no conditioning, no advice, no support. It would be disastrous. If a coach hasn't engaged with the runners, hasn't helped them train, hasn't recognized their strengths and weaknesses and helped each of them to figure out how to run their leg of the race, his team is going to lose. But too many grantors just want to get it out of the way: write the document, sign it, and forget about it.

One of the reasons for this is that, at the end of the day, transferring wealth is about dying, and who wants to talk about that? Who wants to think about the reality that at some point I'm not going to be here? (I know one person who, when he talks about these things, says, "If I die …") Who wants to think about their parents not being around anymore? Who wants to think about the document that governs the end of life? So, grantors take the personality out of the relationship, saying that you're going to be governed by this piece of paper rather than be engaged with me as an individual. Because that's a tough conversation to have. And without a sense of how to do it, it seems much easier to just avoid it altogether and let the executor and trustee deal with it.

But not having that conversation is like handing a runner a document describing the race she's about to run while she's in the starting block. All of the opportunity to coach, to help and support and advise, is lost. That's why the grantor needs to initiate conversations about wealth transfer, about how each inheritor wants to run their leg of the race, about how the family can win the race by operating as a team. This whole book is really about having that productive conversation about what matters to the grantor, what matters to the next generation, what the family's values are, and so on. The whole family is in the race. What each inheritor does with the legacy is their leg of the race, and they need to own it. And I believe that this should be a conversation about opportunity, not about consumption.

The great thing about having the conversation now is that both grantor and inheritor benefit. The grantor sees the money at work in the next generation—or, at least, has a sense of how that generation plans to use the inheritance—and the inheritors have time to consider how they want to take advantage of the opportunity the inheritance presents. I know it's been satisfying for my father to see how his children have done this, and now that my children are grown, I'm beginning to enjoy that satisfaction, too—because I'm working with them to make the most of their inheritance. (I also advise families to make charitable bequests while still alive, so they can have the satisfaction of seeing their money at work, making the world a better place, and celebrating that as a family.)

If someone said to me, "Steve, if you were going to wake up 150 years from now and could ask one question that would determine for you if the family legacy has perpetuated in a way that satisfies you, what would it be?" it wouldn't be "Does my family have more money now than it did when I died?" It would be, "Has everyone throughout the generations of my family lived a fulfilled life, a life of value, a life that endeavored to have a positive impact on our family and our society?" If I woke up 150 years from now and the answer to that question was "Yes," I could turn back over and say, "Okay, wake me up in another 150 years." The only way I could continue the ball rolling in that direction for my family is by having "the conversation" on an ongoing basis with my heirs. And that's why I'm glad I've done that.

So, don't wait until the next generation to run the race is already in the starting blocks—or, even worse, halfway down the track—to have the conversation about wealth transfer. This is the kind of conversation that can help prevent your inheritors from experiencing wealth as a burden or a stigma, as something that puts pressure on them, instead of providing them with creative opportunities.

The Creative Opportunities That Wealth Provides

The opportunities that having access to family wealth could include things such as starting a business, engaging in advanced academic study, pursuing a career in the arts, starting a venture that could have a positive impact on society—in fact, the opportunities are legion. One of the greatest things about inherited wealth is that it provides a safety net that enables inheritors to take risks that others aren't able to take. It gave me the opportunity to start my own financial firm. It's allowing one of my daughters to dedicate herself to establishing a professional career in music—which is her passion.

Doing things like this with money is so much more satisfying than conspicuous consumption for its own sake, and most inheritors, if given the opportunity to explore what they love to do and experiment with it, will come to the same conclusion. So, this approach is good for the whole family; it advances the family name, not just its fortune. In terms of inheritors running their legs of the relay race, I like to think of the family wealth as providing the equipment—the running clothes, the shoes and socks—and the advanced athletic training that will enable runners to perform at their peak, helping the family win its race and get to the top of the podium.

One of the ways a family can provide creative opportunities for inheritors is to establish what is known as a "family bank." If a family cares about investing in a way that has a positive impact on society while earning positive returns for future generations, it can establish a review committee to make loans to family members. Such a committee is usually made up of family members and nonfamily members (people who either donate their time or are compensated for their time), and the committee can, as on the TV show *Shark Tank*, consider business proposals from the family members and decide whether the family should back the venture. They would both challenge the business plan and, if they approved of it, help get the venture started.

For example, if I was on such a committee and had a nephew who was trying to start up a technology business the committee thought had potential, I know plenty of people in the technology business he could get advice from and could introduce him to those people. Even before that, during the consideration phase, I could tap those people to review my nephew's business plan to see if it was sound. So the family bank involves both financial and human support.

If it turns out that a family member's business proposal can satisfy an underwriting standard, the family bank can make a loan at market rate, helping the family member get financed for a business that a bank or venture capital firm might not be willing to underwrite. This perpetuates the entrepreneurial spirit in the family, establishes accountability for family members, and earns money for the family. If the grantor of wealth creates a family bank committee during their lifetime that can look at both debt and equity for family business enterprises, they will see the results of that investment while still alive.

> *One of the greatest things about inherited wealth is that it provides a safety net that enables inheritors to take risks*

My father believed that what I was building at Pathstone was going to be beneficial to our family, so he trusted me and believed in my abilities and invested in me. He studied the business and challenged it and looked at who I was partnering with and came to the conclusion that it was a sound investment for our family's money. And he was right! So, the whole family enjoys and celebrates our successful venture.

This kind of creative use of family resources, this kind of sound investment in family members' ventures, can be a win-win situation. I see iterations of this in my work, where there is good communication about and honest analysis of the investment of family funds in business ventures. Just recently, I worked with another father and son who are starting a new venture together. And they are leveraging the family office that we've established for them for accounting assistance and due diligence and documentation—what we call governance. But the education, the comradery, the striving together to build something that comes from this father and son working with one another—that's using wealth as opportunity. If the wealth just gets handed from one generation to another with no sense of legacy, no plan, no dialogue, no taking passions into account, that wealth will just be depleted. There are so many ways to leverage wealth as opportunity. This doesn't mean it's not available for consumption, for pure enjoyment. It just means that it's there for more as well, to perpetuate opportunity rather than to simply be consumed.

I don't want to give consumption a completely bad name here. Being able to use wealth to enjoy life is a wonderful thing. Some wealthy people just feel guilty about their ability to consume. James Grubman, the author of *Strangers in Paradise: How Families Adapt to Wealth across Generations*, suggests a more balanced approach:

> For those who take an avoidance [of consumption] approach, they too believe the stereotypes of the rich ... They say, "We don't want to be like those people. Even though we have money, we're not going to act rich." But, their view of acting rich is, again, that stereotype they've seen in movies, or books, or TV.

> A better strategy is a middle ground, which is letting go of the stereotypes of what it's like to be wealthy. Realizing ... that you can have money. You can be relaxed and make thoughtful choices about it, including sometimes being willing to spend it without

automatically falling into extravagance and materialism in a way that loses your values.[4]

Having family conversations about the use of wealth will help you establish the family values you want to respect as you put your wealth to use.

---

4   "A Conversation on the Perils of Wealth Avoidance," Fidelity Family Office Services publication, n.d.

CHAPTER 3

A SAFETY NET SUPPORTS CREATIVE RISK-TAKING

We all know that rewards don't come without risks. Depending on the endeavor, there can be risks to health, reputation, relationships, self-esteem, and, of course, finances. The choices we make about what we do with our life—what we work at (or don't work at), what we put our time into—have an impact on what life is like for us and for others in our family. Wealth is a tremendous opportunity because it can provide a safety net that reduces some of the financial risk for what we choose to do—and if grantors and inheritors have "the conversation" that I've been referring to throughout this book, they can also reduce the personal risks involved in making a choice.

The dialogue between the grantor and the inheritors provides an opportunity for the experienced veteran to coach those who will run the next leg of the relay race. The grantor is well along on their leg of the race (remember, you don't want to wait until your leg is finished) and has a good deal of wisdom to share about running the race successfully. The veteran can describe the risks and help the rookies avoid them or learn how to handle them. The veteran can ask questions such as, "Have you thought about this?" "Are you worried about that?" and then provide reassurance.

The idea is for the inheritors to be aware of the risks of each opportunity they are considering, then to choose one and develop a good plan, a vision that is both practical and exciting. This is a key coaching exercise for the grantor and a key learning exercise for the inheritors. This is how risks can be considered and overcome or reduced. But the conversation shouldn't just focus on risks. It should also be a celebration of the opportunity, a celebration of each inheritor's passion and how they want to follow that passion with the support of the family. If this is done, when inheritors follow those passions and begin their ventures, they will be well informed, well coached, well supported. They'll be able to take risks, push the envelope, because of their safety net. Those risks need to be well considered, but they can be taken with less fear of an unsuccessful outcome.

The Three Cs of the Safety Net

Through my personal and professional experience, I've learned that an effective safety net is made up of three elements, which I call the Three Cs: capital, confidence, and connections. As you can see, only one of those elements, capital, is about money, so if the focus of a grantor is only on transferring money, the safety net will have significant—and dangerous—holes in it. Let's talk about what each of these three components of the safety net is all about.

Capital

Instead of consuming all the capital in a personal fortune, a grantor can use it creatively while still alive to support the ambitions, dreams, and passions of inheritors. How it's distributed is up to the grantor, but it's important that the distribution be done after exploring how the wealth might be used by those inheritors. What kind of projects or activities do they have in mind? What will they cost? Will they increase the family's wealth or contribute to the family's advancement in some less tangible way?

Remember that the inheritors are "rookies." They're about to run a leg of the relay race for the first time, so they need the benefit of a veteran's wisdom. The grantor has usually been dealing with capital for a long time and knows more about how to use it wisely. The ideal situation is for the grantor and inheritors to work together to determine how much money is needed, when it's needed, how it will be distributed, and if it needs to be paid back, and if so, how.

Part of the ability of inheritors to take risks is that there's capital there to serve their needs, the financial needs of the whole family. But it's important to have a conversation about exactly what the risks entail, about what it means to have a budget, about the kind of lifestyle that the inheritor wants to live while pursuing a passion with family capital. My father had this conversation with me when I approached him about starting a financial business with family capital. Having been an entrepreneur himself, he had a lot of hard-won experience to share with me about what is required financially and emotionally to start a business. Listening to what I wanted to do, and drawing on that experience, he was able to help me determine how much capital I needed and how I should go about using it. And I'm doing a similar thing with my own children.

Not all grantors will have experience with the kind of projects that inheritors want to pursue—for example, one of my daughters is pursuing a career in music, an industry I know little about—so they will need other advisors to participate in the conversation. The family bank and review committee structure I described is one way of providing that guidance.

I mentioned that you need to consider how the inheritor wants to live while pursuing a project. There is lots of published wisdom on the subject of what an acceptable draw rate is on a pool of capital, about how much capital can be used without reducing the buying power of the next generation or, God forbid, depleting the principal of the family fortune. But inheritors should also be able to enjoy their wealth, within reason. Let's say that a reasonable annual draw rate on a family's $100 million of wealth is 3.5 percent, which is $3.5 million. Does that mean that inheritors should go out and spend $3.5 million every year, just because it's available? Of course not. Part of the conversation about capital use should be about what "feels right," what is the proper balance between using the capital for projects (businesses, education, philanthropy, etc.) and using it for things such as a large home and exotic vacations. My father made our life very comfortable as we were growing up, but he never overdid it in his use of money on lifestyle. We had nice homes. We had nice vacations. But it never felt excessive.

I've invited my own family to think about how they live, and all families should do this. What's the nature of their community? What is it they want to accomplish? Say one of them wants to do advanced academic study. How much capital does it take to provide safe and secure shelter, healthcare, food, engagement with community, and so on? And that should be part of every conversation about how much capital is needed. Then the grantor and each inheritor should develop a budget that's built on what feels right. But there should also be enough available for extracurricular enjoyment, because humans don't live by work alone. Again, it's that need for balance. You don't want an inheritor to stand still with the baton, to just spend every cent available and not advance the family in any way, because that will make it harder for succeeding generations. The family is a team that should be focused on winning, to get to the top of the podium together.

It's great when an inheritor's project is something that will increase family capital, but I don't believe that this should be a requirement of inheritance. If an inheritor identifies their contribution to society, their path to personal fulfillment, as being a schoolteacher or a nurse or a writer or a social worker, and that is how they want to run their leg of the race to feel personally fulfilled, the family should have that covered—that should be recognized as a legitimate use of the capital that is available.

Certainly, no one should feel so pressured to increase the family capital that they resort to semilegal, illegal, or exploitive means to accomplish that. That would be akin to a runner in a relay race injecting performance-enhancing drugs or cheating in some other way in order to win. The goal is always to increase the family's wealth in ways that are morally good for the individual as well as helpful to society.

Confidence

A family of wealth should empower its members to succeed. And they should celebrate effort as much as outcomes. In my estimation, and in my experience, this is a very important aspect of the safety net, because it inspires inheritors, motivates them to do their best—just the way the members of a good relay team cheer each other on. The message to each inheritor should be "I'm confident about you and what you're doing. I believe in your efforts." It's important to separate efforts from outcome, because in many cases in life, the outcome has an element of luck in it.

People say you make your own luck, but sometimes that's just not possible. A good business idea can fail if it happens to come along at the wrong time. A musician composing really good original music can fail if the public isn't ready for that music. A philanthropy established in another country can fail its mission if the government restricts its efforts. There are all kinds of unpredictable things that can go wrong with an inheritor's project. So, what the grantor and family have to look at is the inheritor's passion, engagement, drive, and work ethic, and then celebrate the effort being put in.

> **A family of wealth should empower its members to succeed. And they should celebrate effort as much as outcomes**

It shouldn't just be about making money. You can lose money and still develop a skill or uncover an opportunity or learn what not to do in the future, which are all valuable lessons. Let's say an inheritor has started a drug company and is going through clinical trials for a drug to cure cancer. Maybe they don't succeed economically because they run through their research funding before they get to clinical approvals, or maybe there are still imperfections in the drug that prevent it from getting approval. But maybe the biotechnology they developed is picked up by a future developer and something great is done with it. That's a highly valuable outcome, even if it wasn't financially successful for the inheritor.

It's not just the financial outcome that determines success. There are also these questions: What has the inheritor done to perpetuate the family reputation and legacy? What have they done to strengthen family relationships by partnering for a good cause? For me and my dad and me and my wife and kids, and for many other client families I've worked with, what we've found is that the journey is as important as the destination.

I've talked about how much confidence my father had in me, and his confidence in me made me confident in myself. If a savvy entrepreneur and businessman such as him believed in what I wanted to do, how could I not believe in it? I was too young to understand the dollars and cents involved in successful entrepreneurship, but having the example of his passion, energy, engagement, and success, I came to believe that I could succeed as an entrepreneur. I had seen him succeed, and he believed that I could succeed, so it really seemed possible.

This drove me to work hard to maximize the opportunity he was giving me. But he was also comfortable with the possibility of my business failing. He made it clear that my good reputation with him would not be tainted if things didn't work out. And that made me more comfortable with that possibility. He also understood the amount of money and the kind of connections I would need to have a chance of making my business fly, so he provided a great deal of practical, as well as emotional, support. And I'm trying to do the same for my kids as they begin to run their leg of the race. The side benefit of consulting with my father about what I wanted to do with my life—which, in this case, was starting a business—was that we got to know one another better. And the same has happened with me and my kids. It's a tremendous benefit that one can't put a price on.

There's this concept of kicking the bird out of the nest, hoping that it will fly, but as far as I'm concerned, that's leaving too much up to chance. If all you do is kick the bird out of the nest, you reduce the chances that the bird is going to learn to be successful at flying. So, it's not just about kicking the birds out of the nest; it's teaching the birds to fly and even flying along with them for a period of time, until they're confident enough to fly solo.

If all a grantor does is drop a bunch of money on inheritors and stand back passively to watch what they do with it, the grantor loses the opportunity to get to know the inheritors better and to instill confidence in them. And getting to know the inheritors better helps the grantor understand how to advise and support the inheritors as they figure out what they want to do with their life and their inherited wealth. It enables the grantor to perpetuate the family's values and ensure the family's legacy.

A grantor may find that kicking the birds out of the nest, just giving them enough capital to try flying on their own, may end up perpetuating the financial capital of the family (although I think the chances of inheritors succeeding financially will be smaller). But even if they do succeed financially, the grantor will have missed out on the real value of consulting with inheritors, which is making that personal con-nection and enhancing the unity and purpose of the family as a whole.

My kids know they can count on my confidence and support every day. I provide that for them, just as my father provided it for me. They know I'm cheering them on, on a daily basis, that I'm engaged with what they're doing. I talk with them often enough to understand the nuances of what they're doing. I've invested capital, yes, but I've also invested personal time and effort getting to know what drives them, what they want to achieve. And I'm proud of them each time they achieve a goal they've set. And I know my dad's engaged with what I'm doing, paying attention to what's happening in my business, thinking about where it's going. And I know he's proud of what I've achieved and excited about what else I want to achieve.

I absolutely have a deeper relationship with my father because he engaged with me about handing off the baton, so I could run my leg of the race, and expressed his confidence in me. I absolutely have a deeper connection with my kids because I've engaged with them about my handoff and their leg of the race and have expressed my confidence in them.

The handoff is considered the most difficult part of a relay race, so it's important for those involved in it to slow things down, think about the transition, and figure out the best way to do it. In order for it to succeed, the person handing off the baton and the person receiving it have to work together closely to make it successful—they have to develop confidence in each other. And the same is true of handing off wealth. The families who manage wealth transfer successfully view it as a partnership and a team effort and embrace not just the opportunity presented by wealth as capital but wealth as a subject of dialogue about life.

Connections

As I described in chapter 1, it was an introduction by my father that enabled me to get into the derivatives business right after college, and that was what led to my career in the financial industry. Grantors with wealth and some level of prominence are often connected to people who can help their inheritors get a start in a business or industry. And if the connection isn't direct, they often know people who know people—the old "six degrees of separation" concept. Once again, this is why "the conversation" is so important. The more grantors know about their inheritors' passions and goals, the more likely they are to be able to connect them with people who can be helpful.

My daughter Julia is a musician, and my wife's friend is prominent in the music world as a composer, arranger, and performer. When he heard that Julia was writing her own songs, he was kind enough to ask to listen to some of her work. As it turned out, he was genuinely enthusiastic about what she had done—enough that he took an interest in her career and they have subsequently enjoyed sharing notes on pieces, and Julia even was invited to visit him in his studio. My daughter Heather wanted to move from acting to entertainment law, and I was able to connect her with a banker who worked in entertainment, and he was able to connect her with people prominent in entertainment law. They not only made it clear what the business was about but recognized her passion for the work and encouraged her. The support of these people has helped both Julia and Heather feel confident about what they're doing with their lives, because it was confirmation of their talent and passion from professionals in their fields, not just from their family—which we all need.

The connections that can be made might not even be for a job or even an internship. They might just involve getting sound advice from an experienced person about a business an inheritor is considering going into. In this situation, it is very useful to have access to someone engaged in that line of business. The inheritor has a passionate interest in business but needs guidance, advice, and perspective about what that business is really like and what it demands. The ability to leverage a family's network to find such a person means that the inheritor will enter the business—if their interest survives learning about the reality of that business—with eyes wide open, so there will be less risk of unpleasant surprises.

A connection can even result in someone mentoring an inheritor in the pursuit of a career or building a business. That level of support makes it even less likely that the inheritor will fail. Being in a family of wealth and prominence makes it more likely that inheritors will have access, or be able to get access, to someone who can guide them through the early years of following their passion.

To return to my relay team metaphor, having a safety net is like being on a relay team for a major university, rather than for a small college. Because of a major university's reputation for success, you're going to have more confidence being on their team and more motivation to live up to the expectations for a team at this level. Because the major university's athletic program has more capital behind it, you're going to have superior coaching, equipment, facilities, and physical training. And because the staff is more likely to be prominent in the relay-racing world, they're more likely to be able to connect you with, say, an Olympic track coach, who might consider you for the Olympic Games. (In the more popular sports, major universities are often pipelines to lucrative athletic careers.) So, there are just advantages inherent to being associated with such an institution.

An effective safety net provides all three of these things, too: confidence, capital, and connections. Each is important, and each should be taken into account in the grantor-inheritor dialogue. That dialogue communicates to the next generation that their passions are being heard and appreciated. It expresses the grantor's confidence in them. If the grantor is investing in an inheritor, providing the means to succeed, it demonstrates more than just, "Okay, I'm allowing you to do this." It's demonstrating confidence in the inheritor's passion for, and engagement with, whatever they want to accomplish in life. And what grows from that should be a wonderful, fulfilling conversation between the generations, where the grantor seeks to empower the inheritor's success in the world.

CHAPTER 4

MAKING IT TO THE TOP OF THE PODIUM

The goal of this book is to teach you how grantors can work with individual inheritors to help each of them get to the top of the podium, and how each generation can work with the next to get a whole family to the top. I think I've already made it clear that I see the top of the podium in this race not only in financial terms, but also in terms of individual and family satisfaction and positive impact on the world. It's not that the goal itself is new. Most grantors would like to achieve what I've described in this book, but in order to do it, they must know what to look for in their inheritors and how to work with them so that each individual and the family as a whole can win the race.

The approach I recommend for discerning what your inheritors want to do, and taking advantage of that knowledge, can be summed up in the three words *talent*, *opportunity*, and *passion*—TOP. It is the confluence of these three elements that reveals what an inheritor ought to do with an inheritance and with the family support that should go along with that inheritance. Let's consider what each of these elements means and how it plays into "the conversation" and the relationship between grantor and inheritors.

A side note here: Let's keep in mind that not everyone is going to display talent and passion and be capable of seizing opportunities right out of the starting block. They may require someone to be inquisitive and supportive and patient to help them find what they're capable of (or potentially capable of), what they really care about, and how they can find ways to develop their capabilities and exercise their passion.

An acquaintance of mine told me a story about a kid at a progressive school in Massachusetts, where they believed that kids would find their passion on their own, if given the opportunity to explore whatever they wanted to explore and the advice and support of the staff. The staff would hold classes in math or art or science or any subject whenever a group of kids decided they wanted to learn about something. They were also there to consult with the kids as they were figuring out what they were passionate about. One kid spent years fishing in the pond on the school's property. He would ask teachers about one thing or another over those years, but he spent most of his time fishing and thinking about who he was and what he wanted to do with his life. Just when his parents were about to despair over the school's approach, the kid came to realize that computers were his passion. He started, with the help of his teachers, to study computer technology. He was so passionate about this that by the time he was a teenager, he was able to start his own computer consulting and troubleshooting company for consumers and made a success of the business. It took him a long time, but he ultimately found his passion.

So, you never know what's going on inside a kid's head, and sometimes it will require real patience to find out.

In the following sections I'll discuss each of the TOP approaches to working with inheritors, but please forgive me for the order. I want to discuss opportunity last.

Talent

This could be called the bottom line for a grantor's and/or family's decision about whether an inheritor's career choice is viable. Let's say Chad wants to be a professional golfer, and maybe he's even a really good golfer by family standards—maybe he wins every extended family tournament in a family of decent golfers. His desire to go professional may seem reasonable. But if he hires a good coach and practices avidly for years, but fails time and again, year after year, to qualify for the professional tour, Chad and the grantor or family will need to reconsider whether he has the actual talent to be a professional golfer, even if he has the passion—and, because of family wealth, the opportunity—to pursue that passion. This doesn't mean Chad has to abandon his passion for golf, but it may mean that he has to be realistic and realize that golf may not work as a career for him.

This is not to say that talent will necessarily manifest itself immediately. It's possible, especially at a younger age, that there is a seed of raw talent that, if nurtured, will develop into a significant talent. And that nurturing can be part of what family wealth enables an inheritor to do. But ultimately there comes a point where someone outside the family, someone objective, someone knowledgeable about the art or business or field of study being pursued by the inheritor, has to weigh in about whether the pursuit is a reasonable one for that inheritor, whether there is reasonable hope for success.

The situation with my daughter, which I mentioned in the previous chapter, where her stepmother and I helped make a connection with someone prominent in the music world, is a case in point. We made that connection for her to provide her with a realistic picture of the music world, but what it led to was this musician hearing her perform and recognizing her talent, confirming that her pursuit of music as a career was not just realistic but a very good idea. Earlier in her life, this had been confirmed by professional musicians who taught her—that was another step along the way—but the confirmation by a popular and successful musician cemented the idea that she had the talent to make it as a professional musician.

My other daughter has a habit of charting her own course, but when she was at a West Coast university studying acting, she decided that she was interested in pursuing a career in entertainment law. She called me about it—not so much to get my approval but because she was passionate about doing this and wanted to share this discovery with me and get me behind it. Ultimately, I was able to get her in touch with some people I knew in entertainment law—again, to help her get a realistic picture of what the work would be like. She learned about that from them, but she also got confirmation from them that she had the kind of skills, attitude, and experience with the arts that would be effective in the practice of entertainment law. So, she transferred from that West Coast school to an Ivy League institution in the Northeast, where she graduated with honors. I think the reason she was successful—besides the fact that she's my daughter and is incredibly smart—was because she believed she had the talent to pursue that area of study and that career.

But what do you do if an inheritor doesn't know what their talent is and doesn't feel passionate about anything in particular? This is where the grantor and other family members can help. There can be a dialogue that focuses on helping the inheritor become more conscious of who they are; what talents have been displayed, even if only in the form of potential; and what ideas or activities have ignited a spark of passion. Even if a kid is only sitting on the couch playing video games, well, find out what excites them about video games. What would take advantage of the quick intelligence and/or hand dexterity that being good at video games displays? This is just an example, but it's this kind of thinking, this kind of creative dialogue, that can help an inheritor begin to explore how they want to run their leg of the race.

Passion

I'll talk about passion next, because, like talent, it is not something that the outside world can provide but something that needs to be inside the inheritor and strong enough to carry that person through all the stages that will get them to the top. Passion without talent might actually get an individual somewhere, because intense dedication goes a long way, but talent without passion will not go anywhere. A talent will not be developed, will not grow, will not get itself in front of the world if the individual with that talent has little passion for the thing they are good at. So it is essential for a grantor to dialogue with inheritors to determine what kind of projects or work they are passionate about—and to take it to heart when they discern those passions.

A story about my musician daughter and me at a pivotal point in her life conveys what I mean about listening for the passion and supporting it. She was midway through her

> *It is essential for a grantor to dialogue with inheritors to determine what kind of projects ... they are passionate about*

sophomore year at a university in New York City, studying music. She was getting good grades and was somewhat engaged with her music program, but the program was not evoking her passion. Her dissatisfaction culminated in a call to me from the middle of Washington Square Park. It was late at night. She was crying. And she said, "Dad, this isn't getting me to where I want to go."

I asked her to tell me more about that. And she said something like, "I expected more from this community. I wanted more. I expected people to be more engaged with music, more passionate about it. I just wanted more. And I'm not getting it here. I really think I've got to change direction. I want to get back to the kind of directed learning I was doing outside of school before I came here. I want to study privately with some local musicians I respect. I really feel like this is the time. I'm afraid if I don't do it now, if I just plod along in this school experience, I'm going to lose the energy, the momentum, the passion I have about music."

I asked her what she wanted to do, and she said she wanted to suspend her studies—not suspend her engagement with her craft or with developing her musical talent, but just her formal studies. And she wanted my support for doing this. And I told her that, for me, there is no greater gift for a parent than to be able to support a clear talent and passion in a child, a talent and passion that can lead to a lifetime of fulfillment. And I said to her, "It's clear to me that you are connecting your talent with your passion, and the path to doing that doesn't always follow step by step the way we think it will."

This was a great opportunity for me, as both a parent and a grantor, to support my inheritor's talent and passion, and help her navigate the path to developing that talent and passion. This was a real "passing the baton" moment for us, because she was telling me how she felt she needed to run her leg of the race. And I take pride and joy in the fact that I was able, in that moment, to really hear her saying, "This is what I need, right now, and I want you to help me get there." It was a powerful moment of mutual trust, mutual engagement. She was defining her legacy, and I needed to support that effort. I needed to communicate that I believed she could do it, that I would support her trying, that we should make it happen and map out this new opportunity.

So, that's what we did, and that moment set her on a path to deeper learning about music and greater success as a musician. She followed the independent path she needed to at that time—the path dictated by her passion—and eventually decided that she wanted to complete a music degree and study more deeply, but in a community where there was a higher level of engagement. So, she transferred to Berklee College of Music in Boston, from which she will graduate while I'm engaged in writing this book—on a subject I'm passionate about!

This is the creative and supportive role that a grantor can play in the life of their inheritors. It offers so much more than just providing them with a lot of money or demanding that they follow a path the grantor wants them to follow, which might have nothing to do with their own passions. A *Boston Globe* article published on December 25, 2021, described the approach to passing the baton taken by Sewanee Hunt, a very wealthy baby boomer:

> Hunt doesn't think she should dictate how her heirs make their impact in the world. She has a message for the younger generation—and for her fellow boomer activists: Rather than pick up and run with the elders' causes, she said, "Do the next right thing. The danger is when we try to make the next generation look like us, care about the same things. The spark may go out."[5]

---

5   Robert Weisman, "In a Turbulent Time, Baby Boomers Are Set to Pass Unprecedented Wealth to Younger Generations," *Boston Globe*, December 25, 2021.

I couldn't have put it better myself. Whether you're "activists" or have some other orientation toward the world, don't let the spark go out in your family in the next generation. Listen to your inheritors and keep it glowing!

Opportunity

Once inheritors have identified their talents and passions, they need opportunities to develop those talents and apply their passions. Grantors can provide some opportunities, of course, by investing directly in inheritors' education or training or projects or businesses. And I've also talked above about how families of wealth often have connections that can provide such opportunities for inheritors, whether it's helping them get an internship or connecting them with someone in a particular industry for informational talks or suggesting additional investors who might be interested in a project. This is where families can work together and be creative to help one of their members pursue a dream.

And sometimes opportunities just come along and must be seized. My becoming the CEO of a wealth management firm was that kind of opportunity, as I've mentioned previously. As head of the Braverman family office, I had approached a national wealth management firm (one of the few that existed at the time) for help with managing certain aspects of my family's wealth—which did not include investment advice, which I thought I could handle better myself. They came back to me and asked what I thought of their wealth management approach from an investment advisory perspective. So, I told them frankly that the approach we were taking in our family office was a bit more advanced than what they were doing.

This company was owned by a bank, and I told them that they had a conservative, banker's investment advisory approach, whereas my family office had a more entrepreneurial approach—and, frankly, we got better results with our approach. Two weeks later, they came back to me and said they'd thought about what I'd told them and agreed with it. And, oh, by the way, in addition to being a client, would I be interested in becoming president of the company and building the kind of portfolio-management service I would have bought from them, if they'd had it?

This was not the kind of opportunity likely to come along often—if ever—and it aligned perfectly with what I'd become passionate about. I consulted with my father, and he recognized it as a golden opportunity to extend what I was already doing in wealth management for the family, as well as continuing to manage the family wealth via this company. I was asking him to let a group of strangers get involved with managing our family wealth, when it had just been me and a small staff before, but he was willing to do that to support me. With his blessing, I said yes to this wealth management company. And, ultimately, my current company, Pathstone, grew out of that unusual opportunity.

It takes real belief in yourself and your talents to take advantage of opportunities when they come along, because real opportunities bring real challenges. I had never run a wealth management company before, so I had to believe that I knew enough about what was important in wealth management to lead such a company. I also had to believe in my managerial abilities. Having earlier made the transition from running a trading firm to managing the family wealth, I had developed some confidence in my ability to do new things that aligned with my passion. And having my father support both of those moves boosted my confidence, too.

So, for an individual inheritor, and for the family as a team, getting to the top of the podium in the race requires boldness and confidence and support when opportunities come along. It's like a runner who has a chance to try out some completely new technique, or a team that decides to take a new approach to running a relay. Doing things in a new way, seizing an opportunity, is scary as well as exhilarating, and it takes guts to do it. This is why if inheritors are applying real talents and acting on real passions, they are much more likely to find opportunities and to seize them with enthusiasm.

Talent, opportunity, and passion—TOP: those are the keys to running the best possible race. But in order to move successfully along the right path—in order to stay on course during the race—you also need to be able to measure success along the way. Next, we'll talk about how to do that.

CHAPTER 5

MEASURING RESULTS, STAYING ON COURSE, AND RECOVERING FROM FALLS

I've established that I believe wealth is meant to create opportunity, not just to be consumed. And that when inheritors are thinking about opportunities, they should recognize that they've got this safety net beneath them and understand that what will help them succeed in their leg of the race—and get the family to the top of the podium—is recognizing their talents, opportunities, and passions. And grantors need to communicate with inheritors to learn how the family can help them be what they want to be, to help them define their own legacy and run their leg of the race. So, if you're at that point in "the conversation," the next step is to decide—together—how you'll measure inheritors' individual success—whether that's in monetary terms, or impact on society, or level of happiness with life.

This is the point where the baton gets passed—and as we know from relay racing, the baton handoff is the most difficult part of the race. I look back to my experience with my father as an example of how to do it well. First of all, my dad coached me about the nature of the race I was facing when he told me in college to find my own passion and talent and explore it. This led to my getting into the financial world and succeeding there on my own. Then I suggested using my talents, my expertise in capital markets and financial engineering, to manage and develop our family's wealth. And my father supported that move.

But the real handoff of the baton happened when my father allowed me to commit the family's wealth to the wealth management firm that hired me as its CEO—because then that wealth was more in my hands than in his. We developed a plan for how we would determine if this approach was successful, how we would work together to try to make it successful, and what we would do if the approach wasn't succeeding. But it did succeed, so we never had to make any significant adjustments.

So, there are four steps in this next phase of wealth transfer—which is really the point where the baton is passed and the next generation begins running their leg of the race. Grantors and inheritors need to establish and agree on how these four steps are defined. The steps are as follows:

» Develop a plan.

» Establish roles.

» Measure success.

» Make adjustments.

Let's look at what each of these steps entails.

Develop a Plan

Ben Franklin said that "if you fail to plan, you plan to fail," and I could not agree more. Dispensing wealth willy-nilly, with no concrete plan for how it's going to be used, does a disservice to the grantor, the inheritor, the family, and, ultimately, to society, because people of wealth can have a significant impact on society. I personally believe that this plan should be written—both because writing things down tends to clarify thinking and because a written plan is something you can refer back to. Writing it down is not chiseling it in stone; most plans need adjustments as time passes and further experience is gained. But having a plan written down gives it weight, gives it a sense of reality that a verbal plan can't.

A plan should have goals, of course, and those goals should include small, incremental goals as well as bigger goals and an ultimate goal. I'd like to use my brother David's experience as an example as I talk about each of these steps. His ultimate goal was to become a professional golfer. He was passionate about golf, and it had been established that he had real talent. He'd been successful playing in high school and college, and afterward won some amateur tournaments, and ultimately he became champion of a Florida golf club that hosts PGA tournaments—in fact, posting scores better than some of the professionals who played there. So, he wanted to become a pro, he had the talent, and now he needed a plan to try to achieve that goal.

He sat down with my father, and they devised a plan. My brother agreed to practice every day, outside of his work time. He would get the best instruction available and work hard to implement what he learned from his instructor. He would enter the most challenging tournaments he could get into as an amateur, and if he did well there—a measurement of his success—he would take a year off of work and practice his game full time, aiming to get into the PGA Qualifying School, which would qualify him for PGA tournaments. Finally, he would enter tournaments and see what level of success he could achieve, see if he had what it took to be a professional golfer. The plan was clear and the goals well defined.

A plan needs to define what someone wants, how they'll go about doing it, and how they'll measure their success. It takes into account various possible outcomes. What do you need to think about? What are the steps along the way? The better the plan is defined, the more likely it is to succeed. It also helps to get input from the connections I mentioned in the previous chapter in order to plan realistically. Also think about what you'll do if you don't quite make it to your top goal. This plan should be written out in as much detail as possible— a business plan, an education plan, a training plan, something that describes whatever is necessary each step of the way.

Establish Roles

The "who does what" part of the plan, the roles, can be rather simple—as it was in my brother's situation—or more complicated, if the grantor or others in the family take a more active role in helping an inheritor pursue a dream. If the roles involve doing specific things along the way to help the inheritor pursue a goal, those things should be defined. The roles need to be talked through and understood by all. This is especially important in a family, where relationships can be fraught and damage to those relationships can impact family life for a long time. Any family member who takes a role in an inheritor's project should know exactly what is expected of them so unnecessary misunderstandings don't arise.

The biggest and perhaps most important role of family members, however, is to be cheerleaders. The inheritor should feel the family's support every step of the way. They should celebrate the successful completion of each step along the way and provide support when things get difficult, when there are clear setbacks, and even when a project fails or the inheritor decides to stop pursuing it and go in another direction. If the family has had that all-important dialogue about what kind of life each inheritor wants to pursue, they are much more likely to understand and support one another. The grantor should be the initiator of this dialogue and should help

The biggest and perhaps most important role of family members ... is to be cheerleaders

maintain it over the years—as should everyone in the family. I'll say more about how family support should come into play when I talk about making adjustments to a plan.

In most cases, of course, people outside the family will have roles in the plan, too, providing analysis, direction, guidance, training, perhaps even monetary investment, and so on. My brother needed a golf coach to hone his game for professional-level competition. My daughter needed music teachers to develop her talent. Anyone with a business plan needs to run it by a knowledgeable businessperson in order to make sure it's realistic and complete. This is a place where those family connections I mentioned can be really useful, and where having family wealth to draw on gives inheritors a leg up, because they can afford the very best analysis, guidance, and training, as well as having access to people who can afford to invest in projects. One of the big roles of grantors and other family members when the plan is being shaped is identifying people outside the family who can play roles in executing the plan.

Measure Success

Success or failure needs to be measured—and celebrated or adjusted to—each step of the way. This makes the inheritor accountable, both to themselves and to the family. But I don't mean accountable in a punitive way; I mean it as an indicator of how much the inheritor cares about what they are doing and whether the talent and skills are there to bring ultimate success. If my brother had spent his time hanging out in the clubhouse bar instead of practicing his game and playing rounds of golf, it would have been clear that he did not have the drive required to pursue a career in professional golf. If he had never won a significant amateur tournament, it would have been clear that he didn't have the talent to pursue that career. And he would have been the first to admit both of these things.

The measurements that are applied to an inheritor's life project, whatever that project may be, should be agreed upon between the grantor, the family, and the inheritor. This is an important part of the plan, so it must be discussed and decided by all involved. The discussion itself will help the inheritor clarify what they intend to accomplish incrementally and how it will be clear that they have accomplished each incremental step. Anyone else involved in the project, be it a family member or someone else, needs to be held accountable, too, because in many cases, the inheritor isn't going it alone on the project.

When my father and I agreed to move our family's wealth to the wealth management firm that took me on as their CEO, we agreed to see how things went over a period of time, and then decide together if the company was doing well enough to keep entrusting the family wealth to that company. I was accountable, my new company was accountable, and my father was accountable for managing the family wealth for the benefit of all. My father was handing me the baton by trusting my company with the family wealth, but he also continued to watch over what I was doing—the way a veteran runner watches over a rookie—and measuring my success as a steward of the family's wealth.

At twenty-two years old, my daughter reached a milestone last year—a measure of success—when she had a million people stream her music online. In today's music world, online success is mandatory, so reaching this milestone tells her and her family that she is going in the right direction, that all her passion and training and creative hard work is bearing fruit—that the plan we agreed upon is succeeding. (Oh, and the proud father has to add that she is also frequently recognized around New York City by her online fans.)

Many of the families I work with attain their success with the wealth-transfer process because they take entrepreneurial risks and realistically measure risk and return when inheritors plan how they want to run their leg of the race. They take a well-informed plan and execute it well. And setting measurement points is a key part of their good planning. They don't just accommodate the dreams and desires of inheritors but also look at all of the potential outcomes that can be taken as measures of success or failure.

And rather than calling it a failure point, let's call it an information point, a point where the inheritor realizes that they are not following the right path or the right passion or don't have the inherent talent to accomplish the goals that have been laid out—this time—so it's time to move on to something else. At each information point, the inheritor can decide what kind of adjustment needs to be made.

Make Adjustments

Almost no one's path to a goal, to living a certain kind of life, is without bumps, and it is when one hits those bumps that adjustments need to be made. It might mean a minor adjustment, or it might mean adjusting one's life goal.

My brother's experience pursuing a career in professional golf provides a good example. He won a bunch of amateur tournaments, demonstrating that he had the ability to excel in head-to-head competition and could put together consecutive days of great golf. Then the opportunity came along for him to enter a PGA open tournament, one where if he won one of the three top spots in the qualifying round, he would be admitted to this professional tournament.

As he worked through the day in the qualifying tournament, he found himself challenging for one of the three top spots right up to the eighteenth tee. He was just where he needed to be. And then he put his tee shot out of bounds. But he didn't panic—you might say he handled it like a pro. It was a par five, and he put his second ball in play from where he went out of bounds, with a one-stroke penalty. And he still made par on the hole! Despite this amazing recovery, he missed the cut by one stroke. If it hadn't been for that penalty stroke, he would have had a place in the tournament.

By all accounts, this was an amazing day, where he demonstrated that he was one of the best amateurs in the country and clearly had the right stuff to pursue a professional career. The only adjustment he would have had to make would have been to figure out what went wrong with that tee shot. But, as it turned out, in his mind it was time to make a major adjustment.

When he explained it to us, he said something like, "You know, I interacted with the guys, I talked to them about what the life of a professional golfer is like, and I realized very clearly that it's not what I want. I've worked through my plan, dedicated myself to it. I've demonstrated that I could succeed. But I've seen the life: living out of a car, going from town to town, being away from family for months on end, and I've now realized that this is not what I want to do with my life. I want to be there for my kids and my family. I want to be a great father. And I can't do that living that kind of life."

Now, you might think the family would have been dismayed by this, looked at it as a failure, but we did not. We celebrated with him! Why? Because he'd taken advantage of the opportunity that the family wealth had given him; he'd worked hard at something he was passionate about, and he'd ended up learning something very important about who he was and how he wanted to live his life. This demonstrates what I mean when I say it's not just about the money. It's about the opportunities to experiment, to learn and grow, that the money provides. Who can put a price on learning an important lesson about oneself and one's life? That kind of experience is priceless. Oh, and by the way, my brother turned out to be a great family man!

I also think back to my conversation with my musician daughter, when she got to the point where she felt she needed to adjust her plan for music education. That was a smaller adjustment of the plan—she wasn't abandoning music—but it was big enough that she needed to feel supported by the family when she did it. And here, too, it was all about having a conversation, about listening to what she needed to do to follow her passion. And it was our family's job to support that decision emotionally as well as monetarily. So, we adjusted her plan and, as I've described, that adjustment set her on the right path for developing her music the way she needed to, and that has led to her success as a musician.

Bumps along the way are part of the process, not disasters. A friend of mine told me about hearing the CEO of an innovative, entrepreneurial software company, a former high school math teacher, speak about how he had succeeded when so many other entrepreneurs failed. What he said was that he had succeeded "because I saw every failure as an opportunity." This is the spirit with which every inheritor's plan ought to be approached. If things go wrong, don't give up—unless what you've learned is that you're ready to move on—just adjust and move forward.

It doesn't matter if what the inheritor is pursuing is a business or an individual plan, such as those I've described. If it's a business and it isn't reaching the point of profitability as quickly as expected, then you look at the plan. What internal or external factors kept the business from reaching the planned profitability? What can we control, what kind of adjustments can we make, versus what we can't control— and are those uncontrollable factors too big to overcome? Did we learn something through the process of developing the product or service that indicates we should pivot or reevaluate? Again, there is this concept of partnership, where the family works with the inheritor to find ways to make the plan succeed, or perhaps to admit that it's not going to work out and look to a new project. But even if a project has to be abandoned, what was learned from the failure, how did the inheritor grow, and what is there to celebrate about the experience?

I think about runners looking at their split times and learning from them. Why was I slow out of the block? Why was I faster here than there? What tripped me up on the turn? Learning from races that don't go well is just as important as learning from ones that do go well. And your coach and your teammates ought to be helping you figure out what can be learned from an unsuccessful leg of the race.

Another funny thing about adjustments is that they often have to be made when someone succeeds, too! My success managing the Braverman family wealth led me to having to decide about whether I wanted to take on the CEO position that was offered me. That was a big adjustment. I also had a client who sold their family business for a quarter of a billion dollars. He was a forty-year-old entrepreneur who had led the family business, founded by his mother, to a level of success that made this sale possible. An amazing success, by any standard. But the day after the funds were deposited in his account, he turned to me and said, "Steve, I've never felt so poor." And I said, "We just cashed a check for you for a quarter billion dollars. How can you say that you've never felt so poor?" And he said, "Because today is the first day in my adult life that I'm not earning a paycheck. From this point forward, it's all consumption."

So, even in the face of phenomenal success, this man had a big adjustment to make. Of course, he didn't have to make his life "all consumption" at that point, even if it was possible for him to do that. His adjustment could be to start another company or to found a philanthropic organization. Or he could find creative and satisfying ways to do his consuming of that wealth. But whatever he did, it would be a big adjustment from what he had been doing. Adjustment just comes with the territory of taking advantage of opportunities.

Dealing with Mistakes and the Unexpected

It happens, sometimes. A runner drops the baton. Another runner bumps him off the track. Sometimes the problems that occur are internal—lack of preparation or focus, not practicing enough. And sometimes they are external—slipping on a wet track, being injured. Grantors and inheritors need to deal with both kinds of problems as they plan the use of family wealth, in order to be accountable for the plan they've developed together, in order to steward that wealth responsibly. Any kind of activity in life comes with both risks and the possibility of positive returns. One way you can mitigate risk is by good planning. It also helps to be aware of the kind of mistakes and unexpected occurrences that might happen so you consider them honestly—and that's what I'll cover in this section.

Mistakes

The two most common mistakes that families of wealth make when dealing with inheritors' life plans and goals are as follows:

» Having unrealistic goals

» Setting expectations too low

Let's look at how each of those mistakes plays out.

Having Unrealistic Goals

Let's say a grantor founded a company that was sold for billions of dollars. A lot of factors come into play to make that level of success happen, so it would be unrealistic for the grantor and/or inheritor to expect to match that particular aspect of the legacy that's being inherited. Just because a previous runner on a relay team was capable of setting world records for laps doesn't mean that the rest of the runners will be capable of that—and no one should expect them to be.

Just because someone's father was a Super Bowl–winning NFL quarterback doesn't mean that he is going to be able to win a Super Bowl. Just because someone's mother was a Grammy winner doesn't mean she is going to be able to win a Grammy. Just because the grantor gave a billion dollars to charity doesn't mean that every inheritor is going to be able to match that level of giving. Some

> *One way you can mitigate risk is by good planning*

inheritors even feel that they need to exceed the accomplishments of their grantor—which is a lot of pressure! This is setting oneself up to feel like a failure, instead of being someone who enjoys getting to whatever level of success is achieved.

Grantors and inheritors need to set goals that take the real world into account, not just the insular world of the family community. They need to be realistic so that inheritors aren't bound to fail, because that is certainly not the goal of the race. You don't want to miss the success that actually happens by hiding it behind unrealistic expectations that make real achievements look like failures. No one should have to compete against unrealistic expectations.

Setting Expectations Too Low

People sometimes set the bar too low because they do not want the inheritor to fail. There should be enough accountability to really help the inheritor succeed. And this is not just about the outcome; it's about the journey, too. The expectations for what the inheritor will do to try to achieve the goal should be high enough to make the goal achievable.

As I said, you don't want to set such a high bar that the inheritor is destined to fail, but you also don't want to set it so low that the inheritor doesn't grow and develop and learn something about overcoming life's challenges from the experience. So, it's possible to be too patient with inheritors, to not ask enough of them. And I don't mean just in the context of the outcome, but in the context of the journey to get there. If an inheritor says she wants to be a professional painter, but she's only painting an hour a week, is she really on the path to becoming a professional artist? No. She's painting as a hobby. It's easier to look the other way when this happens, because confronting it will involve a difficult conversation. That's the beauty of a mutually agreed-upon plan, because the grantor can point to that and say, "This is what you said you were going to do, and you're not doing it. Are you still committed to that plan?" There needs to be responsibility and accountability for actions built into the plan.

The Unexpected

There are all kinds of unexpected circumstances that can challenge the best-laid plans. What if an inheritor can't get a handle on their passion? What if an inheritor can't get the help needed to get a project off the ground? What if a health issue comes up? What if a bad relationship makes it difficult for the inheritor to function effectively? What if the economy tanks when an inheritor's new business is trying to get off the ground?

In this section, I'll examine the unexpected issues that I encounter most often when working with families:

> » Family team breakdown
>
> » Lack of a passion to pursue
>
> » Unforeseen economic challenge

Family Team Breakdown

I've described the role of family offices in managing wealth. It's a team of people who manage all of a family's wealth, stewarding that wealth for the family and taking care of financial outputs that need to be made. Naturally, because I run a company that works with family offices, I believe in this approach. But a family office is not a "set it and forget it" kind of operation. It needs to keep up with financial changes in the world.

Let's say that someone sells a business when he's forty-five years old and puts together a well-constructed, dynamic family office predominantly staffed by his contemporaries. Then, fast-forward forty years, so that wealth creator is now eighty-five years old. He's done all the right things in terms of bringing up an empowered family, establishing what the family is about, working with his inheritors to pass the baton, and so on. But everyone in his family office is eighty-plus years old, so they may not be up to speed on the newest, most dynamic ways to manage wealth. In addition, they know the family and its needs well, but that information will retire with them, if no one younger has been brought along over recent years to inherit that knowledge.

If a family doesn't foresee this, there can be a rather sudden and surprising breakdown in the team that is supporting the activities of everyone in the family. And many families don't think about this ahead of time, so when it happens, it feels unexpected. This is the organization that is supposed to maintain the process, the integrity, the culture, and the legacy of the family. For a relay team, the equivalent would be the loss of an important coach, or even a whole coaching staff, or of trying to work with a coach who is past her prime, who is not aware of the latest training and race-running techniques. This puts their team at a disadvantage. To avoid this, a family needs to make sure that its wealth management team is always dynamic, always up to date about wealth management, always ready to serve the family as effectively as possible.

The family team can also break down—or at least be challenged—if there is a member dealing with an addiction or a difficult mental or physical condition. This creates a situation similar to the one I'll talk about next, where there is a family member who chooses not to pursue a passion and advance the baton for the family. In the case of a mental or physical problem, the family member may not have a choice about this, but it would need to be dealt with in a similar fashion, by finding someone to pick up the slack.

Lack of a Passion to Pursue

The fact is, not everyone has a major passion in life, some big goal they want to pursue, some major project they want to take on. There are going to be inheritors whose interpretation of success is not going to advance the baton for the family economically or otherwise. They may try something, discover it requires more time and energy than they want to dedicate to it, and decide to focus on raising a family or on pursuing hobbies or serving their community in some small way. And there's nothing wrong with this. It does not mean that this family member should receive a smaller portion of the wealth that is being distributed. As I said, families should celebrate a member who is pursuing a good, happy life.

But this situation may require someone else, someone who is motivated about the task, to pick up the slack, to steward and advance the family's wealth. It might mean that a family member who is dedicated to this advancement takes on greater responsibility for the family wealth. It might mean that a family member who had not been focused on this kind of task decides to take it on—like a substitute runner or assistant coach in a relay race. However it's done, the family must ensure that someone is stewarding the family's wealth. Others in the family might also need to steward the entrepreneurial spirit of the family, the idea that wealth is an opportunity to do something new, something original.

Faced with an inheritor who doesn't want to be an entrepreneur or advance the baton, a grantor could consider cultivating other members of the family to do these things. For example, the grantor might mentor the children of the inheritor who lacks financial or entrepreneurial drive, if those children have that kind of drive themselves. A grantor may even develop that drive in them, if they're open to it. As I think I've made clear in this book, part of the grantor's responsibility when running their leg of the race is to coach the next generations and ensure that the baton is both advanced and handed off smoothly. The grantor's leg of the race is not over until this has been accomplished.

And if no one is interested in picking up the baton, you can set up a team to ensure that the family legacy endures. I'll discuss this more in the next chapter.

Unforeseen Economic Challenge

Specific economic challenges—recession, depression, rampant inflation, etc.—can't be foreseen, of course, but we all know that such challenges are inevitable, so the first thing to do is create a plan that is designed to survive those challenges.

And, when they occur, inheritors need a team that can be relied on to cope with them, whether it's family members or external advisors with the savvy to do that. Someone needs to continuously monitor the family safety net to make sure it's secure, that it's tight and doesn't have gaping holes. This is another important part of stewardship. You can bet that the woman who is going to walk the high wire checks the safety net before she ventures out on that wire!

So, grantors and inheritors need to ask themselves, "Have we built a solid team? Do we trust our team? Are we engaged enough with our team? Are we engaged enough with the economic situation?" If the tightrope walker falls off the wire and a faulty net doesn't save her, she knows she can't blame somebody else—and if she's killed, that's pointless anyway. The problem was that she didn't engage enough, didn't care enough, to check the condition of the net. So, the key to surviving economic challenges is owning your responsibility for the maintenance of the safety net.

It's all about the Boy Scout motto "Be prepared." Constantly test the safety net and make sure it's still in good condition and doesn't need to be replaced. We talked about trust documents, about grantors feeling that, once they've signed the trust documents, they're done. But they can't do that. They have to regularly go back and check those documents and ensure that they're still in line with current trust laws. And they can't just set the investment components of the safety net and forget them, either. If a grantor bought US bonds at a 5 percent risk-free rate, that investment needs to be adjusted when bonds are yielding only 1.5 percent. So, you need to respect the need for safety, test the safety net regularly. Good pilots check their landing gear before every takeoff—they don't rely on the idea that checking them yesterday means they're still going to work today!

Another aspect of the safety net is how you're set up to react to economic challenges, how capable your team is of converting challenges into opportunities. Ideally, a safety net is constructed in a way that not only allows you to land safely but empowers you to act decisively, to take advantage of changes in the economic environment. A good relay runner will wear one pair of track shoes if a track is dry and another if it's wet, and making that change in response to the conditions will provide an advantage during the race. And even if you just manage to survive a major economic challenge—such as inflation, a market crash, a social crisis—your safety net needs to be constructed in such a way that, once the crisis is passed, the family wealth continues to grow.

It's inevitable. There will be mistakes and unexpected challenges as you run your relay race. The better you plan, the less likely it is that either mistakes or the unexpected will throw you off track, because you will have contingency plans for dealing with them. The planning must include clearly establishing the required roles, measuring success along the way, and making adjustments. With this approach, your family is more likely to win the race and get to the top of the podium.

CHAPTER 6

NOW WHAT?

At some point, you will come toward the end of your leg of the race or you'll finish it, and at that point you might wonder what's next. I mentioned the entrepreneur who sold his family's company and then realized that he didn't have to get up for work the next day, didn't have a workplace to go to anymore. Sometimes things wind down more gradually, but as things are winding down or ending, you need to consider where you're going to apply your energy next. When it comes to wealth transfer, this is a critical phase, and I think there are several things you should do at this point:

> » Celebrate.
>
> » Communicate and engage.
>
> » Perpetuate.

Let's look at each of these and what it involves.

Celebrate

So, you set certain success goals at the beginning of your leg of the race, and you've measured yourself against them, using honest, realistic metrics, and you find that, lo and behold, you've finished your leg, you've succeeded, you've achieved what you wanted to achieve, and maybe more. Now what? At this point, the first thing you should do is take a great deal of pride in what you've done, in the impact you've had on the world, in the way you've helped your family win the race, and you should celebrate it—take a victory lap, so to speak! And while you circle the track, consider all the things that you've learned and accomplished and enjoyed along the way—including things you may not have expected to be part of the experience: personal growth and development, new insights into yourself and life, and so on. Sometimes, we get so caught up in what we're doing that we forget to celebrate what we've already done. And those accomplishments deserve celebration.

I take great pride in what we've developed at my company, Pathstone. We set out to build a premier family office and wealth management organization, and judging by financial metrics, the rapidity of our growth, client satisfaction, and industry awards, we've succeeded at doing just that. And we celebrate it. We feel great about the people we've positively impacted along the way. And, in addition to the personal pride I take in this achievement, I also enjoy the pride of my father, my wife, my children, and my friends. Those are things worth celebrating!

So, enjoy looking back on the leg of the race you've run. Reflect back on the stages of your success, progress, and growth, on the people you've served and the friends you've made. What's the good of doing something great if you never take the time to celebrate and enjoy what you've achieved?

And it's not just about financial success. In some cases, depending on the kind of passion you followed, it may not be about financial success at all. It might be about what you created or about how many people you helped—equally valuable goals that having family wealth makes it easier for you to dedicate yourself to. So, reflect on what a gift that wealth has been, too. Which brings up the subject of wealth as a gift to the next generation.

Communicate and Engage

These activities are intertwined. I've talked about communication with your inheritors throughout this book, and, really, that's not something that should just be starting as you end your leg of the race. However, when you don't need to focus on your leg of the race as intently as you do when you've just been handed the baton, it's easier to create opportunities to communicate and engage with the next generation, the people to whom you're passing the baton. If you haven't done it yet, you can help your inheritors identify their passions and, once that's done, mentor them, coach them as they run their leg of the race, do all the things that help advance them—and consequently the family—in the race. This is the point where the "me" of running your own leg of the race becomes the "we" of helping advance the whole family. It's quite possible you'll still be running your own race to some extent, but take more time to focus on the "we" as well.

And always keep in mind that your job is to encourage your inheritors to pursue their own passions. Don't try to force them into the family business—they don't have to run the race the same way you did in order to succeed, so help them succeed on their own terms. I am enjoying this process immensely with my own children. Not only is it helpful to them, but it brings us closer, which means a lot to all of us.

This is the point in the process where your responsibility to the next generation really kicks in. This is the seasoned runner turning to help his young teammates realize their potential. You don't just finish your leg of the race, drop the baton, and walk off the track. You use your experience and knowledge to communicate and engage with the new generation of runners that's coming up behind you.

Sometimes, there is a long period of handing off the baton, a long period of influence and support. It's been that way with my father. Although I'm the day-to-day manager of the family wealth, he still leads the meetings and remains active in the process of managing that wealth. (It's only lately, as he ages, that he's begun to want me to take over more of the family leadership duties.) Often, in a family company, or any company, for that matter—even a company that's sold to someone else—the founder might retire from active, day-to-day running of the organization but will remain on the board or act as a business consultant to the new generation running the company, continuing to communicate and engage with the new owners. This is another way to take responsibility for your legacy, to make sure that what you've created during your leg of the race continues to succeed once you've passed the baton, that the race is won by those who will continue to run it. As I quoted Ben Franklin, "If you fail to plan, then you plan to fail." Don't fail to plan for the successful continuation of the race you've been running.

Perpetuate

Personally, I don't find it all that satisfying to just stop contributing anything to the world and become only a consumer of wealth. There are plenty of wealthy people who could easily spend all of their time traveling around on their private jets, belonging to a dozen country clubs around the world, entertaining themselves with golf or tennis, eating at fine restaurants every meal of the day, and holding lavish parties every weekend. But those are not the kinds of actions that help win the race for their families, that are going to perpetuate their family's legacy, both social and financial. And I don't think most people feel satisfied by that kind of life. It's finding a way to give back, to perpetuate something bigger than yourself, that will provide real satisfaction.

The way we're operating at Pathstone provides a great example of how to perpetuate the good things you've created. We've been engaging with and mentoring our next generation of leaders since the beginning, because we realize that our organization must be built to serve multigenerational families. This means that our firm, like a family, has to be multigenerational, that we need to perpetuate our successful ways of operating with those who will lead the company for the next generation(s) of the families we serve—and also listen to them about what might be different for their generation. Anybody who hires a family office is basically saying, "Here's all our money, forever. Take good care of it for us." That's a huge responsibility— and honor—and we take that responsibility seriously throughout our organization, from the oldest employees to the youngest, from the current leaders to those who will take over from those leaders. We have a responsibility to perpetuate a multigenerational firm, because we've accepted a multigenerational mandate.

Families have an opportunity to do the same thing. Instead of doing nothing but consuming the family wealth, they can perpetuate it. Instead of tainting the family name, or ignoring its significance, they can perpetuate a legacy of success and/or caring and/or creativity. With my own family, I am putting together a team that will be capable of perpetuating our wealth into the next generation (I'll talk more about this in the next section of this chapter). And many of us are perpetuating the Braverman family legacy of philanthropy, donating generously to the charities that are meaningful to our family, now. The next generation may find its own charities, its own ways of giving back to the world, but they will know what kind of organizations and institutions we have supported and why—and may even be involved with those organizations and institutions as young people, which could lead to them perpetuating that legacy. This is part of the education and advice that can be passed on when you communicate and engage with the next generation.

A Wise Counsel Research report on families that successfully managed wealth transfer over generations had this to say about how those families functioned:

> Multi-generational survival is not primarily a financial matter. Many families create great wealth. What our families have done is a second, less public achievement: a conscious decision to commit themselves to creating a great family. They avoid dissolution because they build shared values, commitment, and organization. They also allow family members, or even branches, to leave the family enterprise if they wish.[6]

It is engaging with one another, talking frankly and listening carefully, that enables families to reach the top of the podium.

Financial Stewardship

Although we've talked about inheritors pursuing satisfaction in ways other than maintaining and increasing family wealth, it is certainly ideal to have someone in the family who is stewarding the wealth— because it's the wealth that creates the safety net for everyone. As I've

---

6   Dennis T. Jaffe, "Good Fortune: Building a Hundred-Year Family Enterprise," Wise Counsel Research, August 2013.

said, I've taken on this role in my family. You could say it's part of the leg of the race I've chosen to run, or you could say that it's a second race I'm running simultaneously. I feel I've gotten this right for Heather and Julia, but what about their kids? What is the responsibility and opportunity for the ensuing generations? What are the challenges going to be? What if there's a gap in financial knowledge and intelligent investing activity? The answer is, if this is not well handled, the baton gets dropped.

It is engaging with one another, talking frankly and listening carefully, that enables families to reach the top of the podium

So, I'm also building a team—within Pathstone and outside of it—that will carry on this work if I decide to completely retire someday or when I pass on. It's important to me that future generations of the Braverman family enjoy the same advantages that I and the current generations are enjoying. I have taken this responsibility, and I think someone in every family of wealth ought to do this, or enlist people who can do it for them.

If your family hasn't done this yet, it's important that it be done now. Don't wait for tomorrow. Don't lose the opportunity every day presents to develop the wealth you have to work with. As much as you want to celebrate and support each other's individual passions, you also want to provide the means for the realization of those passions, now and in the future. You need to have good financial administration and work with a thoughtful and trustworthy professional on the perpetuation of your family's wealth. Asset allocation needs to be optimized. Taxes and liquidity need to be considered. Investments need to be constantly reviewed. Investments are an important part of maintaining and increasing wealth, and they need to be cared for in a way that can be made understandable to the family and that allows them to enjoy comfortable consumption of the wealth, without depleting it too much.

At Pathstone, we try to make the investments as transparent as possible to our clients. We don't try to wow them with a complexity that just leaves them scratching their heads. Our goal is to deliver advice and to educate our clients so they are comfortable with and confident about what we're doing with their wealth. Any financial advisor who seems to want to prove that he's smarter than you, and to demonstrate that you can't understand what he's doing with your money, should not be trusted. Years ago, an East Coast clothing store called Simmons used to air funky ads with the owner as spokesperson, but one very intelligent thing he used to say was "An educated consumer is my best customer." That's the attitude you want in anyone who manages your wealth.

Each generation is going to feel differently about what makes them comfortable and confident about perpetuating the family wealth (which is why we do the intergenerational planning at Pathstone that I mentioned). Each generation will steward the family's wealth in its own way, and that's good—as long as they understand that this is the responsibility that goes along with enjoying the benefits of family wealth. Every generation needs to find people who can speak to them about the nuts and bolts of wealth management: budgets, trust structures, risk and return on investments, how to respond to changes in the economy, and so on. I currently do this for my family, but I don't as yet see anyone in the next generation who is likely to feel called to that—to develop the necessary expertise and take it on.

That's why I'm building that team to do this for the next generation. This team will have—as all wealth management teams should have—integrity, strong financial skills, longevity, depth and breadth of investing experience, and the ability to communicate clearly so the family becomes the educated consumers they need to be. And some people on this team have already known my daughters since they were little, when team members interacted with them over small financial matters, so my daughters know and trust them. This is one of the advantages of starting to get a team together early, not waiting for an emergency or having it only kick in after the grantor's death. You give the next generation a leg up financially. And someone, or a couple of people, within the family will ultimately have to step up and be the family's liaisons with this wealth management team.

Maintaining financial stewardship is one of the keys to winning the race. You want to win your individual leg of the race, of course, but each of us should contribute to winning the entire race for the family, too. And that involves ensuring that financial stewardship is taken into account. My daughters are going to be successful in the way they're going to be successful and may not perpetuate the financial assets.

There are families that are not as laser focused on perpetuating or growing their financial assets, who are more interested in celebrating the individuals that they are, furthering the success of those individuals and their impact on the world. However, I believe that somebody should be ensuring that the race continues for the next generations, that the financial resources are stewarded for the future. You want everyone to win their leg of the race, but somebody has to make sure that the race continues.

This is something that grantors have more time to do as they approach the end of their leg of the race. Certainly, one answer to the "what now" question could be to focus more on financial stewardship.

As I begin to wind down a bit at Pathstone, I'm consulting more with my father on questions such as "What are we going to do with this trust structure? What are we going to do with that investment?" For example, right now, my father and I are looking into a complex real estate project that we might underwrite. I plan to stay engaged with the family finances when I retire. I don't want to just go play golf all day, become nothing but a consumer. So I plan to continue to be involved with growing our wealth as long as I'm able to be. It's a worthy cause.

CHAPTER 7

WINNING THE RELAY RACE OF LIFE

The most important thing I want to get across about engaging with your inheritors is *do it now*! If what I've said in this book makes sense to you, start putting it into action immediately. You can't start too early, and even if you're further along in your leg of the race than some people are when they do this, you can—and should—still get started. Do as much as you can with the time you have—which is a whole lot better than not doing it at all, leaving everything about wealth transfer to documents that no one will see until you've passed away.

To make a comparison, it's become widely accepted in the wealth management industry that it's more satisfying for clients to make large charitable contributions when they're alive, when they can engage with the organizations they contribute to. In the same way, it's much more satisfying to engage with your inheritors during your lifetime, when you can help and influence them and enjoy them as they follow their passions with the help of your family wealth. (And, speaking of philanthropy, you can even get your inheritors involved with the charitable organizations you donate to when you engage those charities during your lifetime.)

For some wealthy people, the "obligation" of dealing with family wealth—dividing it up, administering it, making complex decisions about it—is a burden. But using the approach I've put forward in this book, you can turn it into a satisfying, even joyful process where you actively engage with your inheritors; help them shape successful, meaningful lives;

> ## Every day can be a new opportunity to have an impact on the next generation

and thereby create a positive legacy that you get to enjoy. And if you approach it in a way that makes it an enjoyable and satisfying activity, instead of it being a burden, there won't be any reason to put it off! Every day can be a new opportunity to have an impact on the next generation. And, take it from me (because I'm experiencing it): with this approach you'll also enjoy a sense of peace, comfort, and calm because you'll know that if something suddenly happens to you, your legacy is established and your inheritors are well taken care of.

The Relay Race in Other Areas of Life

As a last word, I want to encourage you to look at other aspects of life in terms of the relay race metaphor I've put forward in this book. I've described the Pathstone approach to succession, which is a good example of how the relay race metaphor can be applied to business. Matt, Pathstone's current president, whom I'm preparing to become the next CEO, came to the company fresh out of business school. I and the company's other leaders have recognized his talent and encouraged and developed it over a number of years. Along with Matt, there are many other committed young people at Pathstone being groomed to lead the company into a bright future. If the leaders of a business are focused only on running their leg of the race, it is quite possible that they will eventually come to a point where they're out of touch with how younger consumers think and what they want. But if those running their leg of the race pay attention to the younger, less experienced runners, the team will remain strong and continue to win. Executives need to mentor, support, encourage, and educate the next generation in order for a company to adapt to a changing world and remain relevant and successful.

Teachers with students, parents with children, even spouses with each other can use this approach, and it will benefit all of them. Because it's not just about family wealth—that's just one place where this approach is relevant. The goal is to both run your leg of the life race and help anyone you're involved with to develop their own talents and passions. For example, my wife, Veronica, has been a tremendous support to me over the years that I've built Pathstone and stewarded my family's wealth. She is running her own leg of the life race, but, like a good teammate, she has also taken time to listen to and advise me about how to handle various decisions and challenges.

I've talked about my own role in encouraging my daughters to follow their passion, but I've not been the only one to help them along in that way. My daughter Julia had a very encouraging teacher named Charlie at the School of Rock in Teaneck, New Jersey, when she was young. Charlie was pursuing his own music career, but he shared his experience with, and passion for, music with her, encouraging her own passion for music. And, perhaps most importantly, he recognized her talent and helped her transition from doodling around in the basement to being a serious musician, to becoming part of a music community, which helped set her on the path to the success she's achieving now.

My daughter Heather also has an important mentor, named Jeff. As I mentioned earlier, when she was just focusing on being a singer/songwriter, she started to think that she might be interested in entertainment law. Jeff was her own entertainment lawyer, and she consulted him about whether she seemed suited to the work. He not only encouraged her to pursue that career, but he actually hired her to work as a paralegal. This strengthened Heather's commitment to pursue law school, which she will be starting in the fall of 2022.

Few people are capable of running their leg of the race alone. Most of us need the advice and support and encouragement of others, to be given opportunities to learn and grow. If we both look to others, to our "teammates," for those things, and, when we're in the position to do it, provide those things for others we encounter—in our family, at work, in organizations we belong to, in activities we participate in—we can begin to build a world where we're more likely to succeed, and where more and more people around us also have the opportunity to succeed.

ABOUT THE AUTHOR

Steve is a Co-Founder and serves as Co-Chairman of Pathstone, the Modern Family Office, which serves families, family offices, and endowments and foundations. He is a shareholder and a voting member of the firm's Investment Oversight Committee and serves on the firm's executive leadership team. He served as co-CEO from the inception of Pathstone through June 2022. Steve's professional experience extends over twenty-five years of working with family offices and advising families on their wealth.

Prior to Pathstone, Steve served as president of Harris myCFO Investment Advisory Services, LLC, where he had broad national responsibility for all aspects of myCFO's investment platform. Additionally, within the broader Harris enterprise (myCFO's parent company), Steve had the distinction of representing the ultra-high-net-worth market segment on the Senior Management Committee for Harris Private Bank.

Steve is a thought leader and regular contributor to the media on a wide range of subjects regarding high-net-worth families, their investment options and challenges, and the approach to multigenerational wealth management. He has authored a number of white papers highlighting how families of wealth can think about their investment challenges and opportunities.

Under Steve's leadership, Pathstone has received national rec-ognition, including most recently 2022 "Best Multi-Family Office (above $15B)" by Family Wealth Report; 2021 "Best Multi-Family Office $20 Billion and Over" by Private Asset Management; "Top 20 RIA Leaders" by *Financial Planning Magazine*; "Top 300 Financial Advisors" by the *Financial Times*; and "Top 100 Independent RIA's" by *Barron's* magazine.

Outside of his professional commitments, he is actively involved with various not-for-profit organizations with a particular focus in health, wellness, and education. He founded the Braverman Family Executive Wellness Program at Englewood Health, one of New Jersey's leading hospitals. In addition, the Braverman Family Foundation partnered with the Jewish National Fund to dedicate the Braverman Family Riding Arena at the Red Mountain Therapeutic Riding Center. The riding center serves those with disabilities or special needs for the population of small communities in Southern Israel.

Steve is a member of the Institute for Private Investors and the Economic Club of New York and sits on the Advisory Board for the Ultra High-Net-Worth Institute. He holds a bachelor of arts degree in economics from the University of Pennsylvania and attended the Keller Graduate School of Management MBA Finance Program.